FLAMES OF WAR

FORCES

CREDITS

Wayne Turner & Phil Yates
Writers

Victor Pesch
Graphic Design

Peter Simunovich
Editor

John-Paul Brisigotti
Editor

Battlefront Design Studio

Tim Adcock, Evan Allen, James Brown, Blake Coster,Casey Davies, Sean Goodison, Mike Haught, Mike Haycock, Mark Hazell, Matt Parkes, Chris Townley.

Internal Art

Vincent Wai.

CONTENTS

INTRODUCTION

Flames of War

In *Flames Of War* you take on the role of a company commander manoeuvring your troops across the battlefields of World War II. This classic period of warfare is brought to life in your own game room. This book provides the core armies in the form of Intelligence Briefings. These Intelligence Briefings allow you to field US, German, British, and Soviet forces that clashed across Europe in 1944.

To play *Flames Of War* you'll also need the *Flames Of War* rulebook. The rulebook contains all the rules that you need to fight miniature World War II battles.

How this Book Works

This book is divided into sections for each nationality. Each nation has intelligence briefings for tank, mechanised infantry and infantry companies.

Each company has easy-to-use charts, highlighting available platoons that are the fighting units of your company. Each platoon diagram visually displays what troops are included in the platoon. Each platoon entry has the points value, strength, equipment and weapons options, so you can tailor your forces to your needs.

A detailed arsenal at the end of each section describes the specific ratings for your units' infantry teams, guns, vehicles and the weapons they use. From tanks to infantry, this book contains everything you need to get started on your army!

To find out more, visit your local game store, or visit our informative website at ***www.FlamesOfWar.com.***

Flames Of War uses a point system when setting up and playing games. Each platoon has a points value based on its effectiveness in a *Flames Of War* game. Typical games are around 1500 or 1750 points, but are certainly not limited to any value! Play any point value you and your opponent decide. You can play small 600-point games in an hour, or you can play mammoth games using armies that are 3000 or 5000 points or more!

In most *Flames Of War* games you will command a company with several platoons. We will use the following sample force to explain how to select your *Flames Of War* force from this book.

Gepanzerte Panzergrenadierkompanie

A	**Gepanzerte Panzergrenadierkompanie HQ** (Compulsory Headquarters) Company HQ with 2 Panzerfaust SMG teams	85 points
B	**Gepanzerte Panzergrenadier Platoon** (Compulsory Combat Platoon) with 3 Panzergrenadier Squads	220 points
C	**Gepanzerte Panzergrenadier Platoon** (Compulsory Combat Platoon) with 3 Panzergrenadier Squads	220 points
D	**Panzergrenadier Anti-aircraft Gun Platoon** (Weapons Platoon) with 3 Armoured Sd Kfz 10/5 (2cm)	120 points
E	**Panzer Platoon** (Support Platoon) with 4 Panzer IV H tanks	360 points
F	**Assault Gun Platoon** (Support Platoon) with 3 StuG G assault guns	285 points
G	**Artillery Battery** (Support Platoon) with 4 10.5cm leFH18 howitzers	210 points
		Total—1500 points

GEPANZERTE PANZERGRENADIERKOMPANIE

Armoured Infantry Company

Company HQ

The company headquarters platoon is required—you have no command without it! When you choose your force the first thing you must purchase with your points is your company headquarters platoon.

Combat Platoons

Usually, at least two combat platoons are required. Whatever your battle plan requires, the Combat Platoons are the ones you rely upon to get the job done!

Weapons Platoons

Weapons platoons come from your own battalion. They are not required, but can offer your company excellent support, such as machine-guns, mortars, recon and anti-tank weapons.

Support Platoons

Support platoons are loaned to your company by the division. These platoons give you extra support in many forms ranging from tanks to artillery.

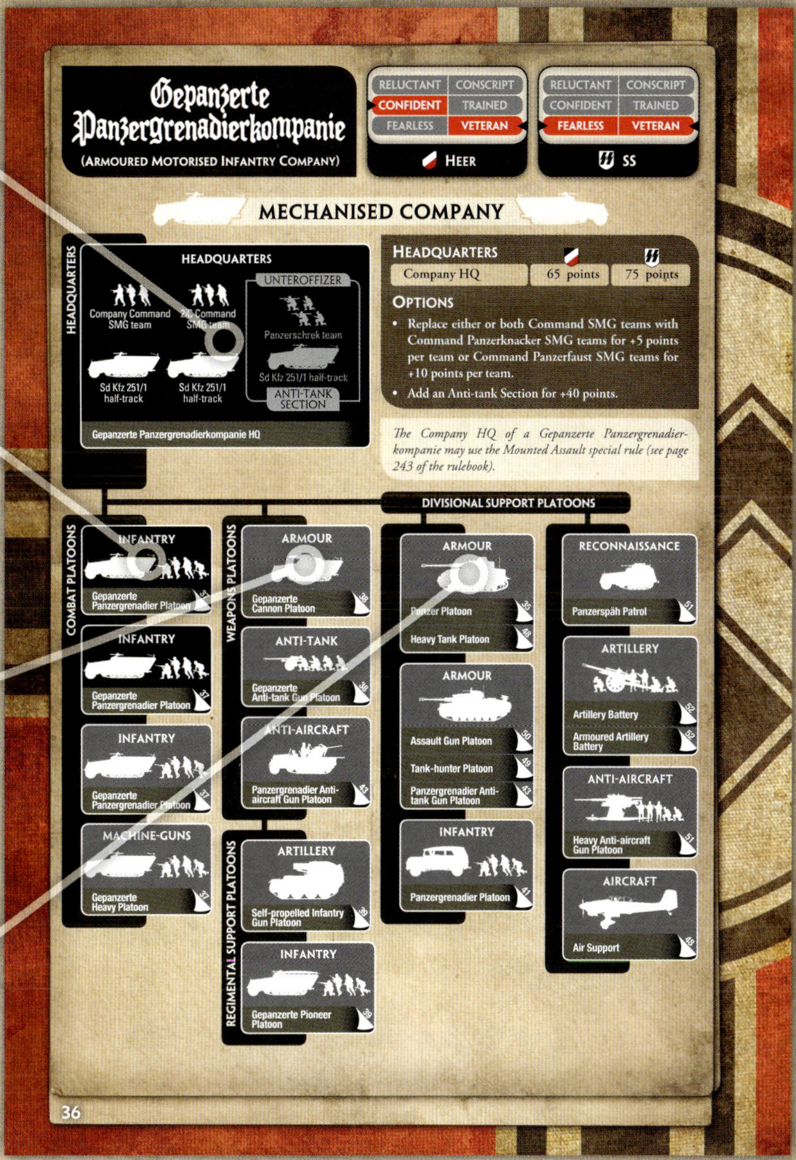

Gepanzerte Panzergrenadierkompanie

(Armoured Motorised Infantry Company)

Heer: Reluctant | Conscript | Confident | Trained | Fearless | Veteran

SS: Reluctant | Conscript | Confident | Trained | Fearless | Veteran

Mechanised Company

Headquarters

Company Command SMG team; 2iC Command SMG team; Sd Kfz 251/1 half-track; Sd Kfz 251/1 half-track

Unteroffizier: Panzerschrek team; Sd Kfz 251/1 half-track — Anti-tank Section

Gepanzerte Panzergrenadierkompanie HQ

Headquarters	Heer	SS
Company HQ	65 points	75 points

Options

- Replace either or both Command SMG teams with Command Panzerknacker SMG teams for +5 points per team or Command Panzerfaust SMG teams for +10 points per team.
- Add an Anti-tank Section for +40 points.

The Company HQ of a Gepanzerte Panzergrenadierkompanie may use the Mounted Assault special rule (see page 243 of the rulebook).

Combat Platoons

- Infantry: Gepanzerte Panzergrenadier Platoon 37
- Infantry: Gepanzerte Panzergrenadier Platoon 37
- Infantry: Gepanzerte Panzergrenadier Platoon 37
- Machine-guns: Gepanzerte Heavy Platoon 37

Weapons Platoons

- Armour: Gepanzerte Cannon Platoon 38
- Anti-tank: Gepanzerte Anti-tank Gun Platoon 38
- Anti-aircraft: Panzergrenadier Anti-aircraft Gun Platoon 43

Regimental Support Platoons

- Artillery: Self-propelled Infantry Gun Platoon 39
- Infantry: Gepanzerte Pioneer Platoon 39

Divisional Support Platoons

- Armour: Panzer Platoon 35; Heavy Tank Platoon 48
- Armour: Assault Gun Platoon 50; Tank-hunter Platoon 49; Panzergrenadier Anti-tank Gun Platoon 43
- Infantry: Panzergrenadier Platoon 41
- Reconnaissance: Panzerspäh Patrol 51
- Artillery: Artillery Battery 52; Armoured Artillery Battery 52
- Anti-aircraft: Heavy Anti-aircraft Gun Platoon 51
- Aircraft: Air Support 48

36

USING A COMPANY DIAGRAM

Each force begins with the Company Diagram, which demonstrates the company organisation graphically in an easy-to-read format. This simple diagram will help you create your ***Flames Of War*** company and get you playing in no time at all!

Choosing your Company

This first step is entirely up to you. There are a wide variety of companies available in ***Flames Of War***, including infantry, mechanised, and tank forces. Have a read through the backgrounds. Find a force that you find interesting and you're off!

Company Ratings and Type

At the top of the first company page you will find Motivation and Skill ratings. The ratings are in red marked with a black arrow. In some cases you may have two variants to choose from. In the example to the right you can either be Heer (rated Confident Veteran) or SS (rated Fearless Veteran).

On this page you will also find the company type. This is used to determine who is the attacker and defender in Missions (see page 257 of the *Flames Of War* rulebook).

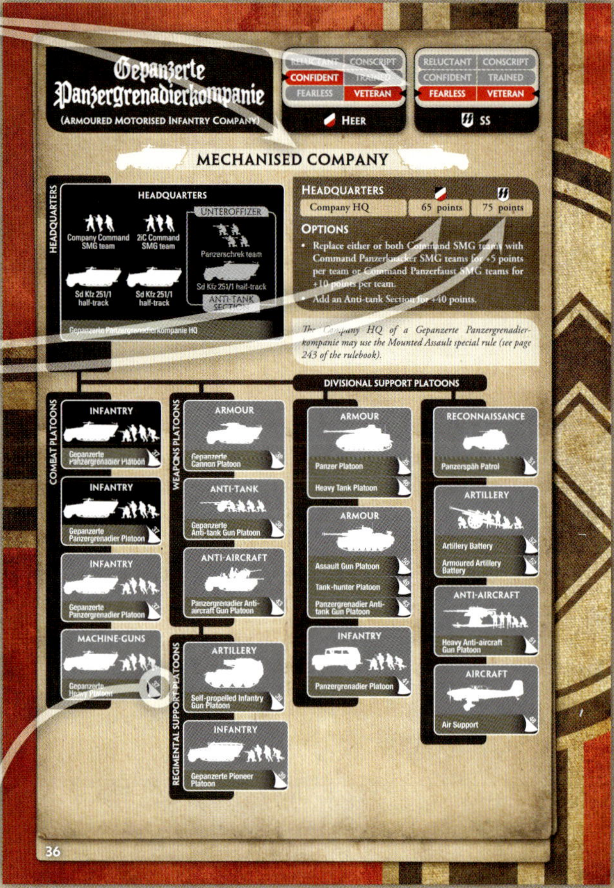

Variant Forces

Some companies are based on a single division or standard organisation, like the Grenadierkompanie. However, other companies have several variants based on specific divisions or branches of the armed forces, such as the Gepanzerte Panzergrenadierkompanie representing *Heer* and *SS* units. These variants may have different support options, as well as different Motivation and Skill ratings. The example to the right tells you that there are two variants: *Heer* (German Army) and *SS* (The Nazi Party's Private Army). When building a force with variants, choose one variant.

When building a force that has several division variants, you must chose one of the variants and stick to it. Your Company HQ and all of your Combat, Weapons, and a few Support platoons must match the division you have chosen. To help, we have included variant symbols to distinguish the variants. Simply use the same variant symbol when calculating points or choosing platoon options.

Building Your Company

You will notice that the Company Diagram consists of several black and grey boxes, each containing a silhouette of soldiers, guns, or vehicles. Each of these boxes are platoons available to your force.

The black boxes are the core of your force. When building your company, you must field one platoon from each box shaded black. The grey boxes are optional platoons. You may field one platoon from each box shaded grey. If the boxes have more that one choice you can only select one platoon from each particular box to field in you force.

Page Reference

Each platoon box will have a page number. Use this to find the platoon and its points value.

Support Platoon Ratings

Divisional support platoons usually have the same Motivation and Skill rating as your force. However, sometimes they may be different. If this is the case their ratings will be given in the Divisional Support section, with the platoon entry, or will be the same rating as the company they come from.

Allied Platoons

Some platoons available to your company are from a completely different nation. These can be easily identified by special national symbols found to the right of the platoon title in the company diagram. Allied platoons follow the Allies rules found on page 70 in the *Flames Of War* rulebook.

Variant Platoon Options

Sometimes a platoon has two or more variant options. These are displayed as separate columns for the points values. In the German section some companies, like the Gepanzerte Panzergrenadierkompanie, can be either *Heer* (marked) or *SS* (marked) above the points column. Within these variants some types of equipment, vehicle or upgrade may only be available to one type. When that option is not available to your variant you will find a dash (-) instead of a points value. This means you cannot take this option.

BUILDING A GEPANZERTE PANZERGRENADIERKOMPANIE

I have chosen to field a Gepanzerte Panzergrenadierkompanie (found on page 36) using the *Heer* (marked [Heer symbol]) variant. I selected this force because of its combination of armoured infantry and tanks.

Reading the instruction under Building Your Company on page 4, I need to field at least a Company HQ and two Gepanzerte Panzergrenadier Platoons in the black boxes. From there I'll add some of the optional platoons in grey boxes. I chose *Heer* (marked [Heer symbol]) as my variant, so all of my combat and weapons platoons should match that symbol.

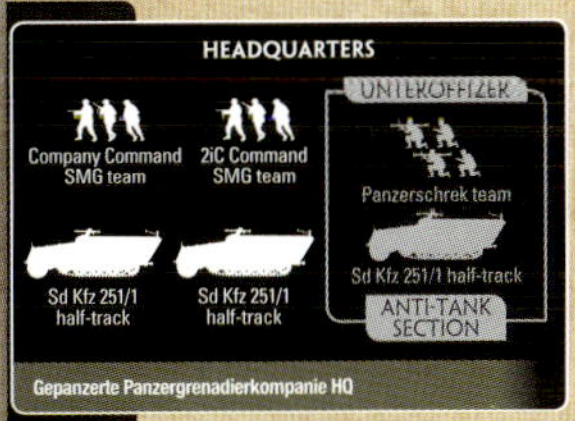

HEADQUARTERS

	Heer	SS
Company HQ	65 points	75 points

OPTIONS

- Replace either or both Command SMG teams with Command Panzerknacker SMG teams for +5 points per team or Command Panzerfaust SMG teams for +10 points per team.
- Add an Anti-tank Section for +40 points.

The Company HQ of a Gepanzerte Panzergrenadierkompanie may use the Mounted Assault special rule (see page 243 of the rulebook).

Many platoons have a list of additional upgrades and replacements listed as Options under the main points. In the case of my Company HQ I decided to upgrade my Company Command SMG and 2iC Command SMG teams to be Panzerfaust SMG teams. For an additional 10 points each I have made these two teams effective anti-tank infantry which should come in handy when fighting alongside my Gepanzerte Panzergrenadier Platoons.

One of the optional Weapons Platoons I would like to take is a Panzergrenadier Anti-aircraft Gun Platoon (page 42). This means I need to use the points listed in the column marked [Heer symbol] to match my variant. There are two available variants: *Heer* and *SS* (marked [SS symbol]). Since I have chosen *Heer* as my variant, I must use the column marked with my symbol (see example below).

PANZERGRENADIER ANTI-AIRCRAFT GUN PLATOON

PLATOON	Heer	SS
3 Sd Kfz 10/5 (2cm)	90 points	95 points
2 Sd Kfz 10/5 (2cm)	60 points	65 points
3 Armoured Sd Kfz 10/5 (2cm)	120 points	135 points
2 Armoured Sd Kfz 10/5 (2cm)	80 points	90 points

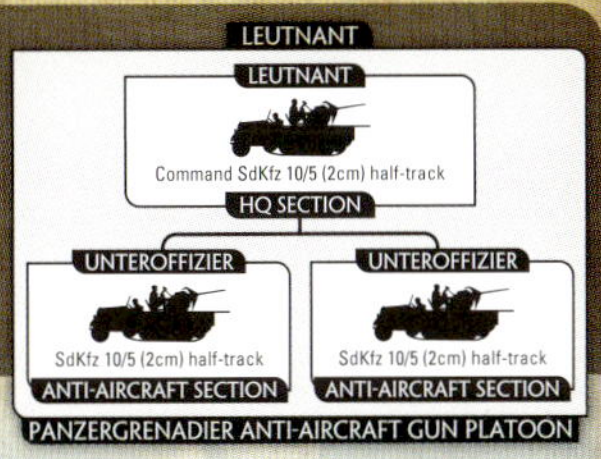

When building my Heer Gepanzerte Panzergrenadierkompanie I use the points in the left column.

I'll need some tanks to help my boys with enemy tanks and to give them some fire support, so I've selected a Panzer Platoon (page 35). Again, there are two available variants, but I have to choose the *Heer* variant. There are also two types to choose from, the excellent Panther tanks and the workhorse of the German Panzer forces, the Panzer IV H. I selected four Panzer IV H tanks as the best bang for my points. While not as heavily armed and armoured as the Panther, it is more than capable of dealing with Allied tanks like the Sherman and T-34.

Next, I would also like to take an Assault Gun Platoon (page 50) to also support my armoured infantry. This platoon can either be *Heer* or *SS*, but as my force is *Heer* I have to take the *Heer* variant. Of the three types available I select the StuG G assault guns as the best option for anti-tank and supporting my infantry. If I had been building a SS (marked [SS symbol]) force I would have only been able to take the StuG G assault guns, as the StuH42 and Brummbär assault guns are only available to the *Heer* (marked [Heer symbol]) variant.

ASSAULT GUN PLATOON

PLATOON	Heer	SS
4 StuG G	380 points	435 points
3 StuG G	285 points	325 points
2 StuG G	190 points	215 points
4 StuH 42	380 points	-
3 StuH 42	285 points	-
2 StuH 42	190 points	-
4 Brummbär	280 points	-
3 Brummbär	210 points	-
2 Brummbär	140 points	-

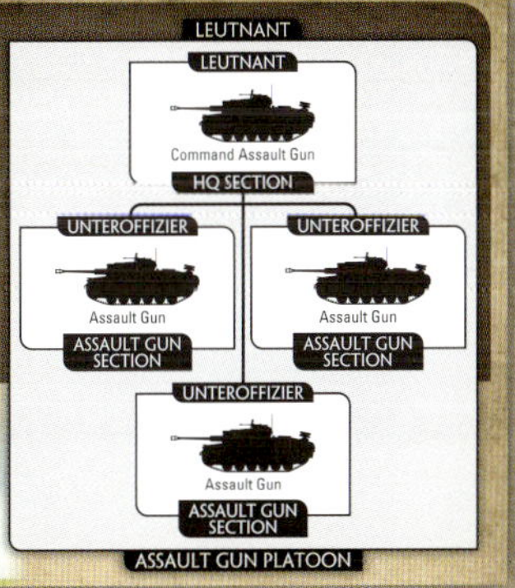

Because StuH42 and Brummbär options have dashes (-) for their SS points column they can't be taken by an SS force.

Finally, I want to add an Artillery Battery. I have two choices: the Artillery Battery with towed guns, or the Armoured Artillery Battery with self-propelled guns. I decided to select the Artillery Battery as I planned to keep them at the back and provide indirect fire support. Once again the Artillery Battery can either be *Heer* or *SS*, so I must take the *Heer* variant. I then have a choice of two types of guns. My battery can either be armed with 10.5cm leFH18 or 15cm sFH18 howitzers. As I had set myself a target points total of 1500 points, I decided to select the 10.5cm leFH18 howitzer option to get close to this target. I took four guns to make my guns their most effective.

ARTILLERY BATTERY

PLATOON HQ Section with:	Heer	SS
4 10.5cm leFH18	210 points	240 points
2 10.5cm leFH18	115 points	130 points
4 15cm leFH18	310 points	360 points
2 15cm leFH18	160 points	185 points

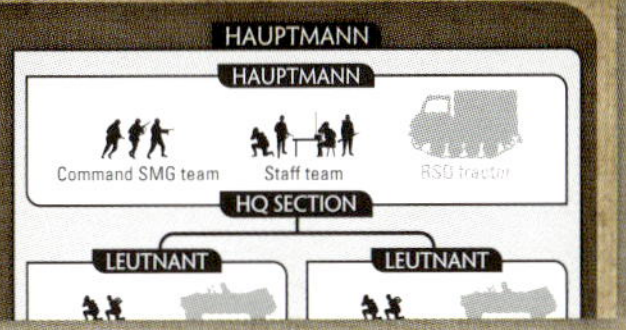

An Artillery Battery can either be equipped with 10.5cm leFH18 or 15cm sFH18 howitzers.

Once I have selected all of my platoons and totalled up my points, I just have to find an opponent with equal points, set up a battlefield and start playing!

VARIANT SYMBOLS AND AIR SUPPORT

When you are building your force often you will have an option to include Air Support. Air Support is usually not marked with a symbol, so when selecting support like in our example above, either option can take Air Support no matter what variant you have chosen.

BASING YOUR ARMY

Battlefront Miniatures packages *Flames Of War* products to give you everything you need to assemble your force as quickly and accurately as possible. Our blisters and box sets are packaged to give you all of the options available to build your army.

HOW TO BASE DIFFERENT TYPES OF UNITS

Every army organises its platoons differently, and the organisation diagrams reflect this. For example, a Panzergrenadier squad in a Gepanzerte Panzergrenadier Platoon is comprised of nine men split into two teams, one of four soldiers and one of five, yet a Panzergrenadier squad in a motorised Panzergrenadier Platoon has eight men split into two teams of four soldiers. Of course, units in combat rarely maintain their theoretical strength. We reflect this by allowing you to take fewer squads.

INFANTRY TEAMS

The fundamental building blocks of an infantry platoon are the various types of infantry teams. The most common ones are shown below with a brief description of their function and organisation.

COMMAND TEAMS

A Command team is made up of an officer, an NCO and a rifleman on a small base. There are often options to upgrade your Command team with a different weapon. To do so, simply replace the rifleman with the chosen upgrade. You can see an example of this on the following page.

RIFLE TEAMS

Rifle teams are the basic form of infantry. All the miniatures in a rifle team will normally be armed with rifles. Some squads may have a single machine-gun, but its effect is diluted by the number of rifles in the squad. Base your rifle teams on a medium base.

RIFLE/MG TEAMS

Rifle/MG teams are organised like rifle teams, except that every squad of two teams has a machine-gun. Base Rifle/MG teams on a medium base with the second base normally modelled with a crew-fed machine-gun.

MG TEAMS

MG teams are better armed than Rifle/MG teams. Every MG team has a machine-gun. Base MG teams with a crew-fed machine-gun and two to three riflemen on a medium base.

SMG TEAMS

Some nations equipped entire platoons with submachine-guns. SMG teams are made up of miniatures armed exclusively with submachine-guns. Base SMG teams on a medium base.

PIONEER TEAMS

A Pioneer team retains the normal characteristics and basing of its type, e.g. a Rifle team on a medium base, and gains combat engineering characteristics and abilities such as an increased anti-tank rating in assault and the ability to clear mines and demolish fortifications.

LIGHT MORTAR TEAMS

Light Mortar teams are made up of a miniature armed with a light mortar and a loader on a small base.

LIGHT ANTI-TANK TEAMS

Light Anti-tank teams are infantry teams made up of miniatures armed with a weapon like a US Bazooka and a loader on a small base.

ANTI-TANK INFANTRY TEAMS

Anti-tank infantry teams are infantry teams made up of two miniatures armed with a weapon like a German Panzerschreck anti-tank rocket launcher and two loaders on a medium base.

GUN TEAMS

Artillery batteries, machine-gun, anti-tank gun, and infantry gun platoons combine command infantry teams with gun teams. Information on basing gun teams can be found on page 12 of the rulebook. Essentially, Man-packed gun teams are mounted like infantry teams on a medium base, anti-tank and infantry guns are mounted on a medium base facing the narrow end, and artillery is mounted on a large base facing the narrow end.

THE PLATOON ENTRY FROM THE BOOK

Each platoon diagram reflects the historical make-up of the platoon and indicates the required squads and teams you must have to make that unit combat-worthy. Troops and vehicles in black are the core of the unit. Troops and vehicles in grey are options that you can add to give them more punch or mobility. Some platoons will list the number of guns or weapons under the 'HQ Section with' heading rather than the number of squads or sections. These points also include any other teams in the diagram in black such as Observers and transports. Many platoons also include options to improve the equipment or capabilities of some of the teams. The platoon entry will also list the special rules that the platoon follows. The platoon entry in a *Flames Of War* book shows you how to base the blister or box set that represents that particular unit. The following example shows a platoon of Panzergrenadiers and how to assemble it using the contents of a *GBX09 Panzergrenadier Platoon (Late)* box.

GEPANZERTE PANZERGRENADIER PLATOON

PLATOON

HQ Section with:

3 Panzergrenadier Squads	220 points	260 points
2 Panzergrenadier Squads	155 points	190 points

OPTIONS

- Replace the Command MG team with a Command Panzerknacker SMG team for +5 points or a Command Panzerfaust SMG team for +10 points.
- Replace Sd Kfz 251/10 (3.7cm) half-track with a Sd Kfz 251/1 half-track at no cost.

Gepanzerte Panzergrenadier Platoons may use the Mounted Assault special rule (see page 243 of the rulebook).

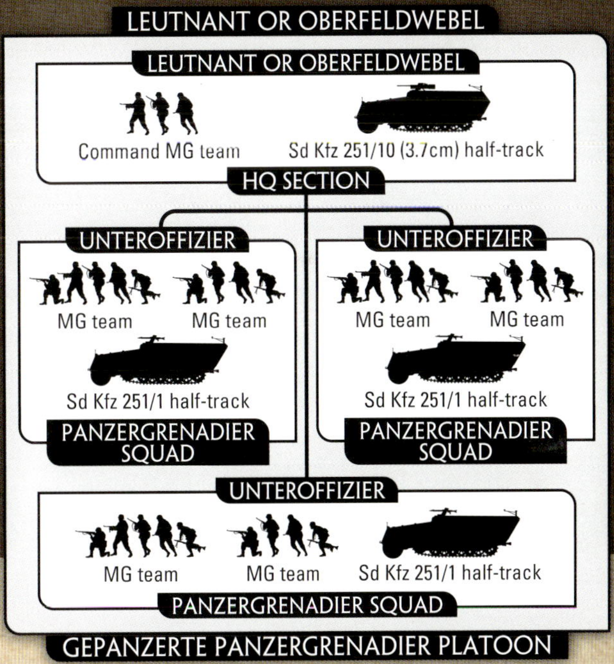

BUILDING THE PLATOON

Use the diagram below to base your platoon. By replacing the rifleman on the Command MG team with a Panzerknacker or Panzerfaust armed miniature, the team is upgraded to a Command Panzerknacker or Panzerfaust SMG team.

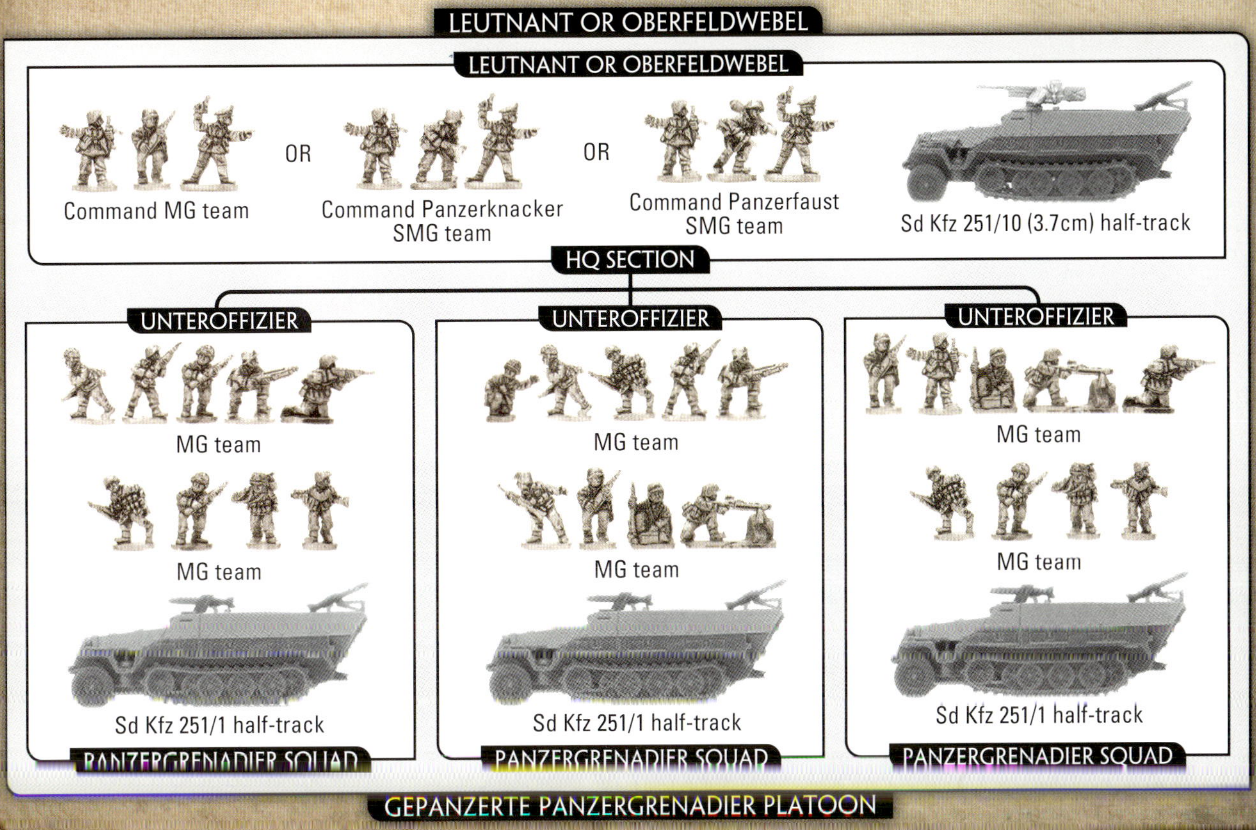

ORGANISATION

It's helpful to know a little bit about military organisation when choosing, researching, and assembling your force. This guide runs through the basic structure of an army and how it relates to your *Flames Of War* force.

ARMY

CORPS

DIVISION

BRIGADE/REGIMENT

BATTALION

COMPANY

PLATOON

SECTION/SQUAD

TEAM

During World War II, every army used a similar structure to organise its troops.

ARMIES

An army is the biggest formation used in most battles. Numbering over 100,000 soldiers, an army is usually made up of two to four corps.

CORPS

A corps of two to four divisions numbers 50,000 to 100,000 soldiers and is usually tasked with a major operation by the army commander.

DIVISIONS

Divisions varied widely in strength from just over 5,000 soldiers to nearly 25,000, but all had a similar organisation with two to four regiments of infantry and one of artillery, along with supporting battalions of all arms. Armoured divisions usually have one armoured regiment and one or two infantry regiments. A division is the smallest permanent all-arms formation.

REGIMENTS AND BRIGADES

A regiment is broken into two to four battalions of the same type with a total strength of 2,000 to 3,000 soldiers.

A brigade is like a regiment, but groups together two to four different battalions (or in British service, two to four battalions from different regiments).

Battalions

A battalion usually has three or four companies and is the biggest force you will usually see on a *Flames Of War* battlefield.

Infantry battalions normally have a heavy weapons company of a dozen machine-guns and four to six mortars (and possibly a few anti-tank guns) as well for a total of 500 to 1,000 soldiers.

Armoured battalions normally have three or four companies of tanks for a total of 40 to 90 tanks.

In addition to their own resources, a battalion-sized task force is usually allocated artillery and tank support from divisional resources.

Companies

The normal force you will field in *Flames Of War* is a company of two to four platoons commanded by a captain or major.

An infantry company numbers between 140 and 240 soldiers. Most of these are riflemen, however many companies have a heavy weapons platoon with extra machine-guns, mortars and anti-tank weapons.

An armoured company is usually equipped with nothing but tanks, having 10 to 20 to its name.

Of course, the battalion commander normally assigns additional support platoons to each company as well, either from its own troops or from the regimental and divisional units assigned to it.

Platoons

A platoon is usually commanded by a lieutenant (pronounced 'loo-tenant' in the US Army and 'left-tenant' in the British Army!), although many platoons were under the command of a senior sergeant. Each platoon has two to four sections or squads, and often a few extra weapons like light mortars and bazookas directly under the platoon commander.

Sections and Squads

The smallest units in any army are its sections or squads. Once again there is a difference in terminology between the US and British Army.

In the US system (used by *Flames Of War*) a squad is a group of 8 to 18 riflemen operating in two or three fire teams, while a section is a single heavy weapon or group of two or three light weapons operating as a unit.

The British Army dispenses with the term squad. Instead it calls everything a section and has them led by a corporal.

TYPICAL ORGANISATION TREE

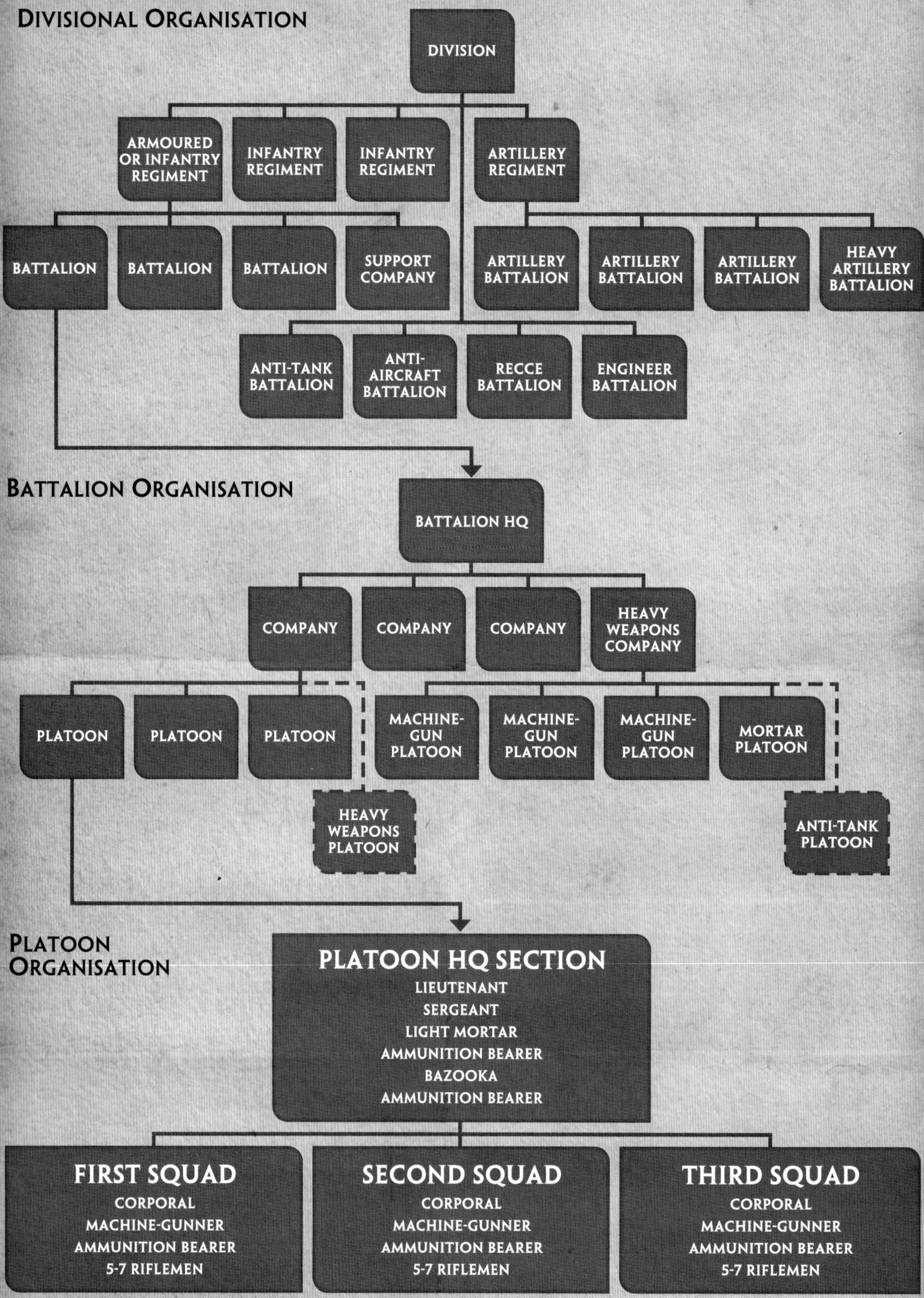

MILITARY RANKS

Military forces are very organised to ensure that everyone has a role and everyone else knows what it is. Once you understand this structure, you can command your forces much easier since you are no longer faced with hundreds of individual soldiers, but rather a few well-organised formations. Everyone knows who is in charge and who they look to for orders.

The table below shows the ranks and roles in the main armies of World War II. You may find this useful when reading the rules or studying the history of this fascinating period.

At the top of the diagram (and the bottom of the heap!) we have the common soldiers. Next we show the non-commissioned officers or NCO's. These are the sergeants and corporals that lead small groups of soldiers. Below that we have the commissioned officers (so called because they hold a commission from their government as opposed to being appointed by other officers like a non-commissioned officer). Officers range from lowly subalterns or junior lieutenants commanding platoons to full-fledged generals commanding armies.

NAMES OF RANKS AND ORGANISATIONS

Number in Command	US Army	German Army	British Army	Soviet Army
1 soldier Basic soldier	**Soldier** PFC (Private First Class)	**Soldat** Grenadier	**Soldier** Private	**Soldat** Krasnoarmyets
3 to 5 soldiers Fire-team leader	**Team** Corporal	**Rotte** Gefreiter	**Group** Lance Corporal	**Otdelenie** Yfreitor
8 to 18 soldiers Squad leader	**Squad or Section** Sergeant	**Gruppe** Unteroffizier	**Section** Corporal	**Sektsiya** Mladshi Serzhant
25 to 50 soldiers Platoon 2iC Platoon leader	**Platoon** Staff Sergeant 2nd Lieutenant	**Zug** Feldwebel Oberfeldwebel	**Platoon or Armoured Troop** Sergeant Second Lieutenant	**Vzvod** Serzhant Leytenant
100 to 200 soldiers Company 2iC Company commander	**Company or Cavalry Troop** 1st Lieutenant Captain	**Kompanie** Leutnant Hauptmann	**Company or Armoured Squadron** Lieutenant or Captain Major	**Rota** Starshi Leytenant Kapitan
500 to 1000 soldiers Battalion 2iC Battalion commander	**Battalion or Cavalry Squadron** Major Lieutenant Colonel	**Bataillon or Abteilung** Major Oberstleutnant	**Battalion or Armoured Regiment** Major Lieutenant Colonel or Colonel	**Batalon** Major Podpolkovnik
2000 to 3000 soldiers Regimental commander	**Regiment or Combat Command** Brigadier General	**Regiment** Oberst	**Brigade** Brigadier	**Polk** Polkovnik
5000 to 25000 soldiers Divisional commander	**Division** Major General	**Division** Generalmajor	**Division** Major General	**Diviziya** General-major

Note: *In many cases officers would command a force larger than their nominal command.*

US FORCES, 1944

'Men, all this stuff you've heard about America not wanting to fight - wanting to stay out of the war, is a lot of horse dung. Americans traditionally love to fight. All real Americans love the sting of battle. When you were kids, you all admired the champion marble shooter, the fastest runner, big league ball players, the toughest boxers. Americans love a winner and will not tolerate a loser. Americans play to win all the time. I wouldn't give a hoot in hell for a man who lost and laughed. That's why Americans have never lost and never will lose a war, because the very thought of losing is hateful to Americans.'

—General George S Patton.

Welcome boys. Good to see y'all. I've got a lot on my plate and some damned gala with the governor tonight so I'll keep this brief. Sit up straight when I'm talking to you son. You're in the army now!

Y'know, it was just a few short years ago, back in '39, that the United States Army amounted to no more'n 174,000 soldiers—all of 'em volunteers. It's hard to believe now, but that's all we had when the War in Europe got started. A paltry nine infantry divisions an' a couple of cavalry ones. We had guns left over from the First War, an' no motorized transport for the GIs.

But there'n that tiny army were some great leaders. Yessiree, men like Generals Eisenhower, Bradley and Patton would forge the US Army into the greatest fightin' force the world has ever seen. They learnt from the mistakes of the Europeans an' came up with a plan to modernize our woefully neglected army. Down Louisiana way in 1940 these fellas organized maneuvers that pioneered the armored tactics we're using to smash the Nazis.

Nowadays we've got an army 91 divisions strong—all of 'em motorized. Maybe the Russkies have got more, but all of ours are at full strength, something no other fightin' nation has been able to achieve.

The US Army fights as a combined arms force of tanks, infantry and artillery—an' I do mean combined. Every infantry division has a battalion of tanks attached, We've got artillery, an' lots of it, at every level. It's kept well supplied so it can fire day and night. It's said the US artillery fires more rounds in a day'n most German units can fire in a whole campaign. We've also got plenty of radios, at all levels of command, meanin' we've got a versatility on the battlefield that the Germans can't hope to match, an' our allies can only dream of.

Now I'm figurin' most of you boys have grown up around a car in the garage tinkerin' with engines and mechanical devices, I'll bet you're all handy when it comes to fixin' stuff. An' what's more besides, here in the good ol' US of A we also value a little thing called freedom, an' no doubt you boys are used to thinkin' for yerself. That's why your average Joe'll make such a good soldier, he can think on his feet and adapt to changin' situations.

You boys are GI's now. That stands for 'Government Issue'—the letters stamped on all of your gear. The only thing the Government doesn't issue you is a wife!

Every soldier goes to war carrying a rifle, an' here it is—the M1 Garand. Ain't she a beauty! Now this ain't nothin' like

the squirrel rifle yer used to back home. This baby's semi-automatic, an' with eight rounds up the spout you can do a lot of very quick shootin'. Backing you up'll be machine guns an' mortars, an' lots of 'em. For each guy on the front line there are at least four guys to support you. Count yourselves lucky. No other army can boast of such a tooth-to-tail ratio, by golly.

You've probably heard that our tanks are famous for their fancy engineerin' and easy maintenance. Shoot, them scientists have even come up with a new-fangled gyro-stabilization device that lets our tanks fire accurately while on the move. An' move they do, on tracks so tough a tank can go for hundreds of miles 'fore they need replacing. Even when they do need a little bit of work, the quartermaster troops can fix 'em up in no time flat and get 'em back into the battle quicker'n you can say jack lightnin'.

Oh, an' by the way, forget about any rumors you boys may've heard regardin' our tanks being prone to catchin' fire. That's a load of baloney!

None of our mighty fine tanks even existed in 1940. But thanks to our industrial might they were ready for combat in strength by the end of '42, just in time for the landings in North Africa. An' we didn't stop there, with all of our industries in full swing American tanks have been provided under the Lend-Lease deal to the armies of all of our allies.

If you think our tank forces are impressive you should see our artillery. The 'Red Legs' are top dog in the US Army, earning for themselves another monicker 'The King of Battle'. No one, and I mean no one, not the Limeys nor the Russkies can match 'em for laying down heavy and accurate bombardments. We've got all our big guns tied together by Fire Direction Centers that'll open up quickly when a request comes in. Heck, German commanders even reckon that the greatest threat to their ability to conduct operations is an American Lieutenant with a radio 'cos time and time again Nazi counterattacks falter under the curtain of steel rained down by the Red Legs.

Anyhows, that's enough gabbin' from me, time fer you boys to get trainin'. Boy-oh-boy, I almost feel sorry for them poor Krauts seeing as they've gotta face us! We're gonna kick their asses all the way back to Berlin!

TANK COMPANY

RELUCTANT	CONSCRIPT
CONFIDENT	**TRAINED**
FEARLESS	VETERAN

TANK COMPANY

HEADQUARTERS

HEADQUARTERS

Company Command M4A1 Sherman

2iC Command M4A1 Sherman

Tank Company HQ

HEADQUARTERS

Company HQ with:

2 M4A1 Sherman	140 points

OPTION

- Equip one Sherman tank with a dozer blade making it a Bulldozer for +5 points.

COMBAT PLATOONS

ARMOUR
- Tank Platoon (15)
- Tank Platoon (76mm) (15)

ARMOUR
- Tank Platoon (15)

ARMOUR
- Tank Platoon (15)

WEAPONS PLATOONS

ARTILLERY
- Tank Assault Gun Platoon (16)

ARTILLERY
- Armored Mortar Platoon (16)

ARMOUR
- Light Tank Platoon (17)

ARMOUR
- Light Tank Platoon (17)

DIVISIONAL SUPPORT PLATOONS

ARMOUR
- Tank Destroyer Platoon (27)

INFANTRY
- Armored Rifle Platoon (19)
- Parachute Rifle Platoon (17)

INFANTRY
- Armored Rifle Platoon (19)

RECONNAISSANCE
- Cavalry Recon Platoon (26)

ARTILLERY
- Armored Field Artillery Battery (28)

ARTILLERY
- Armored Field Artillery Battery (28)

ANTI-AIRCRAFT
- Anti-aircraft Artillery (Self-propelled) Platoon (29)

AIRCRAFT
- Air Support (26)

COMBAT PLATOONS

TANK PLATOON

PLATOON

5 M4A1 Sherman	345 points
4 M4A1 Sherman	275 points
3 M4A1 Sherman	205 points

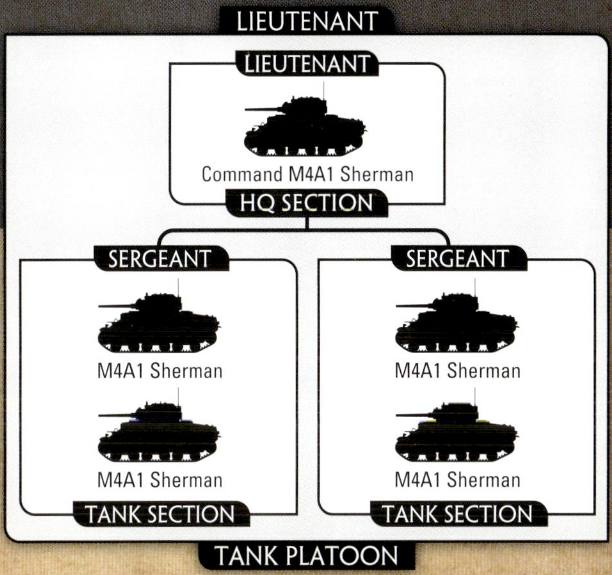

Tank companies represent the mobile component of the US Army. Their task is turning a minor breakthrough into a total defeat for the enemy. Striking with the full power of their guns and armour, the tanks smash through the enemy lines before wreaking havoc within the enemy's vulnerable rear areas, destroying artillery, support units and command centres.

A Tank Company is well equipped for this role having their own assault guns and mortars for artillery support, as well as light Stuart tanks for flank protection.

TANK PLATOON (76MM)

PLATOON

5 M4A1 (76mm) Sherman	445 points
4 M4A1 (76mm) Sherman	355 points
3 M4A1 (76mm) Sherman	265 points

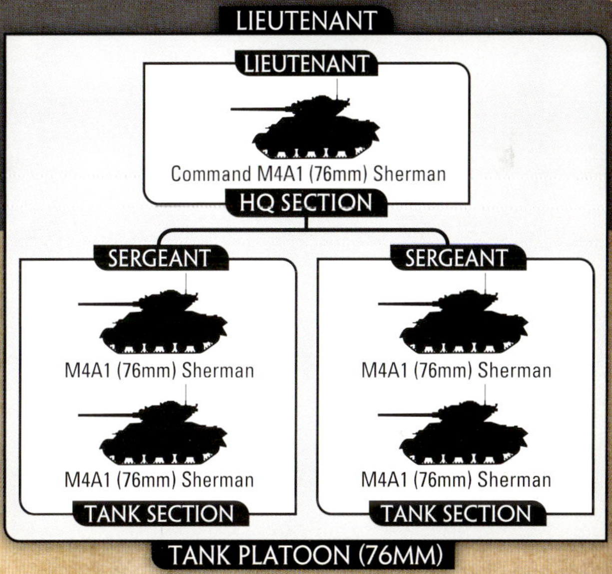

STABILISERS

A stabiliser is a device fitted to the tank's gun that keeps it level when the tank is moving. US tanks are the first in the world to be equipped with gyrostabilisers as standard. With the assistance of the gyrostabiliser, the gunner can stay on target while the tank is moving.

In *Flames Of War* a moving tank fitted with a Stabiliser can fire its main gun at its full ROF instead of ROF 1, but adds a penalty of +1 to the score needed to hit. However, you can choose not to use your Stabiliser at any time if you feel accuracy is more important than rate of fire for the situation.

M4A1 SHERMAN

Armament
M3 75mm gun, Co-ax MG, Hull MG, .50 cal AA MG.

Top Armour: 1
Front Armour: 6
Movement: Standard Tank
Side Armour: 4

Weapon	Range	ROF	AT	FP	Notes
M3 75mm gun	*32"/80cm*	*2*	*10*	*3+*	*Smoke, Stabiliser.*

M4A1 (76MM) SHERMAN

Armament
M1 76mm gun, Co-ax MG, Hull MG, .50 cal AA MG, Protected ammo

Top Armour: 1
Side Armour: 4
Movement: Standard Tank
Front Armour: 7

Weapon	Range	ROF	AT	FP	Notes
M1 76mm gun	*32"/80cm*	*2*	*12*	*3+*	*Stabiliser.*

WEAPONS PLATOONS

Tank Assault Gun Platoon

Platoon

6 M4 (105mm) Sherman	430 points
3 M4 (105mm) Sherman	215 points
2 M4 (105mm) Sherman	145 points

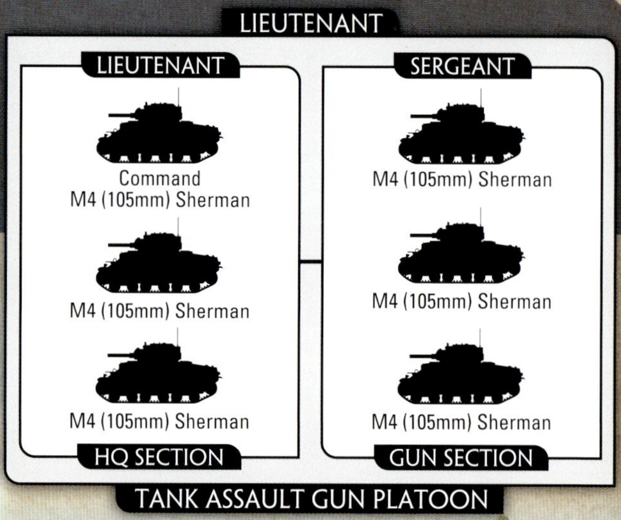

M4 (105mm) Sherman

Armament

M4 105mm howitzer, Co-ax MG, Hull MG, .50 cal AA MG, Protected ammo.

Weapon	Range	ROF	AT	FP	Notes
M4 105mm howitzer	*24"/60cm*	*1*	*9*	*2+*	*Breakthrough gun, Slow traverse, Smoke.*
Firing bombardments	*48"/120cm*	*-*	*4*	*4+*	

Armored Mortar Platoon

Platoon

HQ Section with:

3 M4 81mm MMC	85 points
2 M4 81mm MMC	60 points

Option

- Arm any or all M4 81mm MMC half-tracks with a .50 cal AA MG for +5 points per half-track.

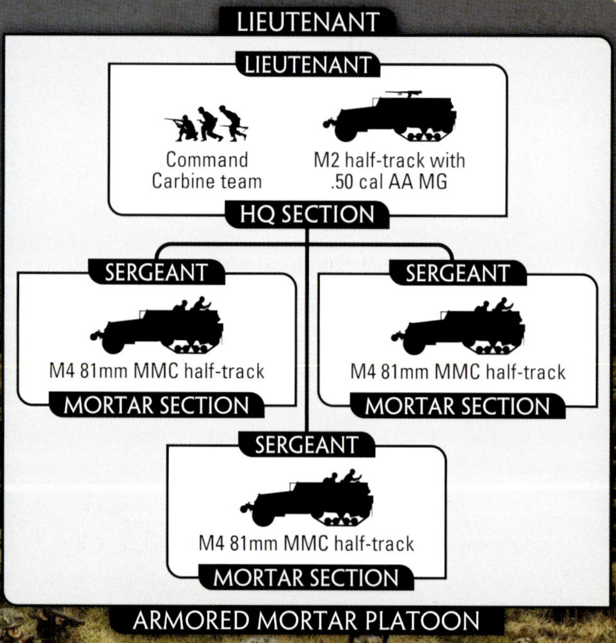

LIGHT TANK PLATOON

PLATOON

5 M5A1 Stuart	235 points
4 M5A1 Stuart	190 points
3 M5A1 Stuart	145 points

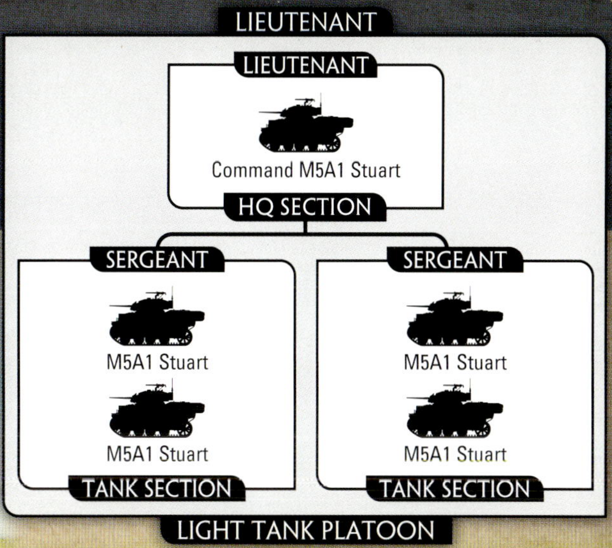

M5A1 STUART

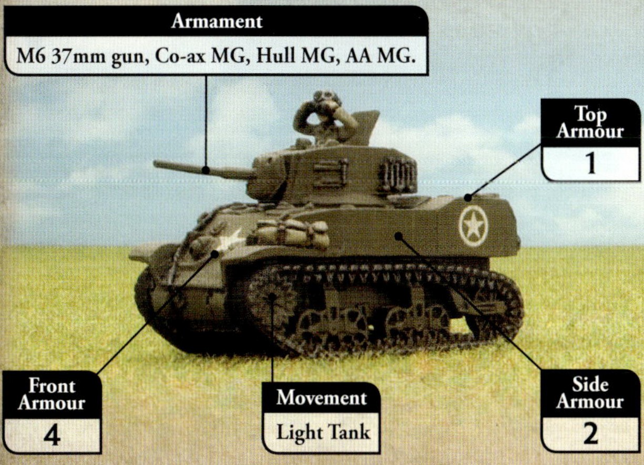

Weapon	*Range*	*ROF*	*AT*	*FP*	*Notes*
M6 37mm gun	*24"/60cm*	*2*	*7*	*4+*	*Stabiliser.*

SUPPORT PLATOON

PARACHUTE RIFLE PLATOON

PLATOON

HQ and Mortar Sections with:

3 Rifle Squads	265 points
2 Rifle Squads	205 points

OPTIONS

- Replace Command Rifle/MG team with Command SMG team at no cost.
- Add an extra Rifle/MG team to all Rifle Squads for +30 points per squad.

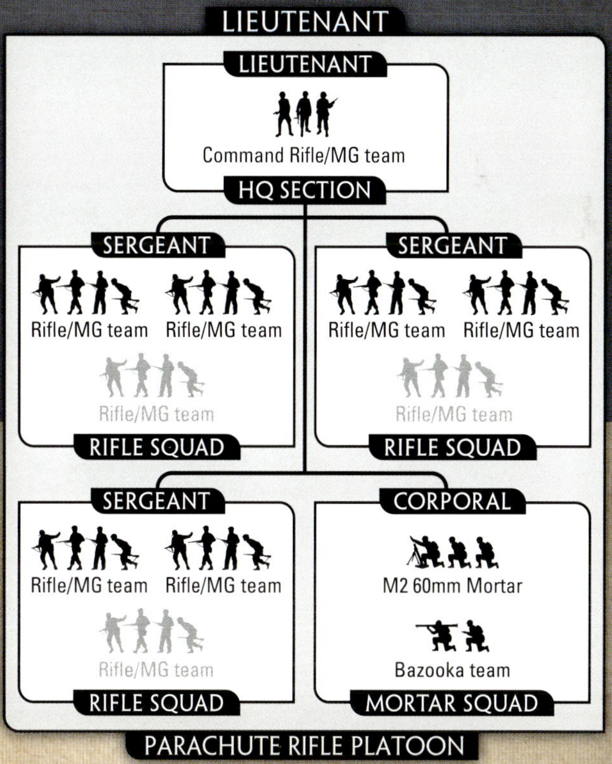

GAMMON BOMBS

All Rifle/MG and SMG teams in the Parachute Rifle Platoon carry Gammon Bombs giving them Tank Assault 3.

MASTER SERGEANT

Parachute missions are tricky and the loss of an officer can result in the failure of the mission. Therefore platoon sergeants are briefed on every detail of the mission in the event their officer is separated from the platoon.

Parachute Rifle Platoons use the German Mission Tactics special rule on page 242 of the Flames Of War rulebook.

Parachute Rifle Platoons are rated **Fearless Veteran.**

ARMORED RIFLE COMPANY

RELUCTANT	CONSCRIPT
CONFIDENT	**TRAINED**
FEARLESS	VETERAN

MECHANISED COMPANY

HEADQUARTERS

HEADQUARTERS
- Company Command Carbine team
- 2iC Command Carbine team
- Bazooka team
- Jeep
- M3 half-track with .50 cal AA MG

Armoured Rifle Company HQ

Headquarters

Company HQ	20 points

Options

- Add a Bazooka team for +15 points.
- Arm the Jeep with an AA MG for +5 points.

The Armored Rifle Company has everything needed to dispatch any foe. Combined with the unmatched mobility they are outstanding in attack and defence.

COMBAT PLATOONS

- INFANTRY — Armored Rifle Platoon 19
- INFANTRY — Armored Rifle Platoon 19
- INFANTRY — Armored Rifle Platoon 19
- ANTI-TANK — Armored Anti-tank Platoon 20

WEAPONS PLATOONS

- RECONNAISSANCE — Recon Platoon 20
- MACHINE-GUNS — Armored Machine-Gun Platoon 21
- ARTILLERY — Armored Mortar Platoon 16
- ARTILLERY — Armored Assault Gun Platoon 21

DIVISIONAL SUPPORT PLATOONS

- ARMOUR — Tank Platoon 15; Light Tank Platoon 17; Tank Destroyer Platoon 27
- ARMOUR — Tank Platoon 15; Light Tank Platoon 17
- RECONNAISSANCE — Cavalry Recon Platoon 26
- ARTILLERY — Armored Field Artillery Battery 28
- ARTILLERY — Armored Field Artillery Battery 28
- ANTI-AIRCRAFT — Anti-aircraft Artillery (Self-propelled) Platoon 29
- AIRCRAFT — Air Support 26

Every Armored Infantry Platoon is an Army

Every Armored Infantry Platoon is like a combined arms force in and of itself. The GI's of the Armored Rifle Company are some of the best-equipped infantry in the world. They have M1919 .30 cal machine-guns, M2 60mm mortars, M3 37mm anti-tank guns, and bazookas aplenty.

The rifleman and all these excellent weapons are carried into battle on the highly mobile M3 half-track that comes with its own .30 cal or .50 cal machine-guns. The half-track machine-guns can be used to provided anti-aircraft cover for the platoon, or dismounted to provided additional machine-gun firepower to the riflemen (see Dismounting Machine-guns on the following page).

The Armored Rifle Platoon's flexibility is the biggest challenge to new lieutenants, as every weapon needs to be coordinated for maximum effect. In attacks the trick is to dismount in cover close to the enemy, set up a base of fire with your machine-guns and mortar, then assault with your riflemen.

While your armoured infantry secure the ground use your supporting tanks to deal with enemy tanks and dug-in machine-guns. Your enemy's will find it hard to repel a well-co-ordinated and supported assault.

COMBAT PLATOONS

ARMORED RIFLE PLATOON

PLATOON

HQ Section with:

Light Machine-gun Squad and 60mm Mortar Squad with 2 Rifle Squads	225 points
Light Machine-gun Squad and 60mm Mortar Squad with 1 Rifle Squad	180 points

OPTION

- Replace M3 37mm gun with a Bazooka team at no cost.

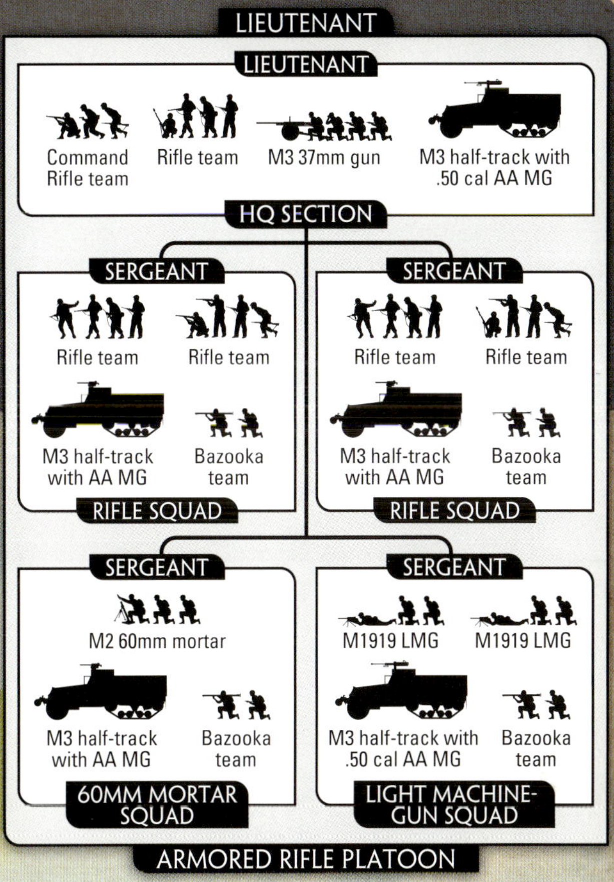

M3 HALF-TRACK

Armament: Passenger-fired AA MG or .50 cal AA MG

Top Armour: 0

Front Armour: 1

Movement: Half-tracked

Side Armour: 0

M2 60MM MORTAR

Notes: Can fire over friendly troops.

Movement: Man-packed

Weapon	Range	ROF	AT	FP
M2 60mm mortar	24"/60cm	2	1	3+
Firing bombardments	32"/80cm	-	1	6

M1919 LMG

Notes: ROF 2 when pinned down or moving.

Movement: Man-packed

Weapon	Range	ROF	AT	FP
M1919 LMG	16"/40cm	5	2	6

MOUNTING AND DISMOUNTING MACHINE-GUNS

Machine-gunners don't just laze around watching the scenery from their armoured half-tracks. Instead, they mount their machine-guns on the sides and blaze away at the enemy as they ride into battle.

Up to two US HMG or LMG teams carried as Passengers in a half-track can fit their machine-guns to the sides of the vehicle, converting them to side-mounted AA MG's (see Mounting HMG's and LMG's on page 237 of the *Flames Of War* rulebook).

Lots of transport vehicles carry anti-aircraft machine-guns. Normally they're left on the vehicle, but when the platoon needs more firepower, they can be taken off the vehicles and fired from a tripod mount.

In *Flames Of War* any US Infantry team carried as a Passenger in a Transport team may Dismount in the Movement Step with the vehicle's Passenger-fired .50 cal AA MG or AA MG (see Dismounting Machine-guns on page 237 of the *Flames Of War* rulebook).

Armored Anti-tank Platoon

Platoon

HQ Section with:

3 M1 57mm	90 points
2 M1 57mm	60 points

Option

- Add up to one Bazooka team per gun for +15 points per team.

M1 57mm Gun

Weapon	Range	ROF	AT	FP
M1 57mm gun	*24"/60cm*	*3*	*10*	*4+*

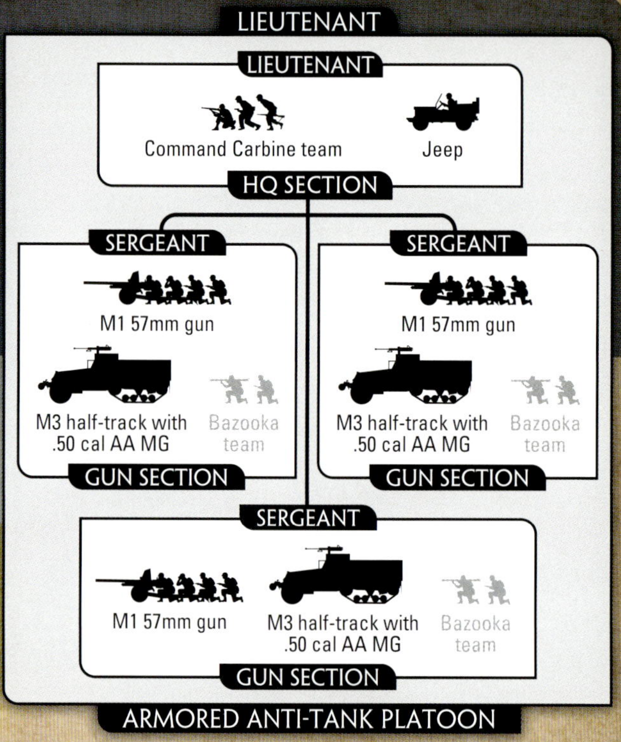

Weapons Platoons

Recon Platoon

Platoon

HQ Section with:

2 Recon Squads	70 points
1 Recon Squad	50 points

Options

- Add a Bazooka team for +15 points.
- Arm any or all Jeeps with an AA MG for +5 points per Jeep.

Recon Platoons are Reconnaissance Platoons (see pages 193 to 195 of the rulebook).

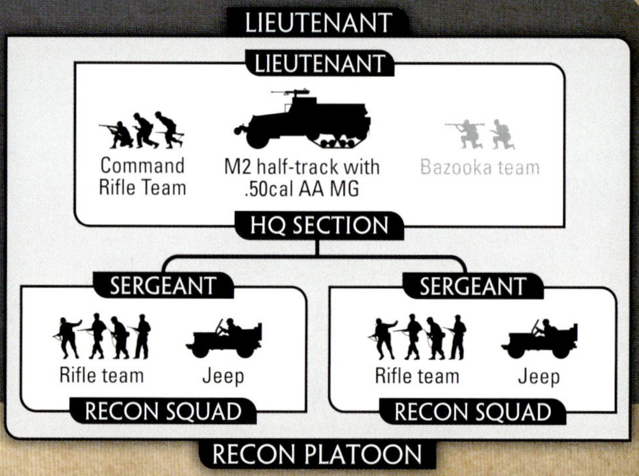

Reconnaissance

Reconnaissance troops play an important role on the battlefield. Whether they are probing the enemy lines for weaknesses, discovering enemy positions, or checking the lines of advance are clear, their success is vital in any operation.

In *Flames Of War* your reconnaissance troops can be equally important. The teams of a Reconnaissance Platoon are Recce teams and this gives them a number of unique abilities in *Flames Of War* (see Reconnaissance on pages 193 to 195 of the *Flames Of War* rulebook).

Cautious Movement

Reconnaissance troops use Cautious Movement. This means that Recce teams that don't move At the Double, carry passengers, shoot or assault in a turn count as Gone to Ground when shot at by the enemy.

Revealing Ambushes

Recce teams also make it harder for the enemy to spring ambushes. The enemy has to reveal their ambushes further away from Recce teams than they would from other troops.

Recce Deployment

Your reconnaissance troops can also probe forward at the beginning of a game with Recce Deployment. This allows you to move your Reconnaissance Platoon before the game begins.

Eye and Ears

Recce teams can also reveal hidden enemy to friendly troops. Eye and Ears allows your Recce teams to take away the Gone to Ground status of enemy platoons with a successful Skill Test, making them easier to hit in shooting.

Disengage

Finally, Reconnaissance Platoons don't over expose themselves to enemy fire and can always Disengage! If successful this allows them to move way from the enemy firing at them before they can get off all their shots.

ARMORED MACHINE-GUN PLATOON

PLATOON

HQ Section with:

4 M1917	105 points
2 M1917	55 points

OPTIONS

- Add one Bazooka team per Machine-gun Section for +15 points per team.
- Add M3 half-tracks with .50cal AA MG to the platoon for +5 points per half-track.

Armored Machine-gun Platoons may make Combat Attachments to Combat Platoons (see page 260 of the rulebook).

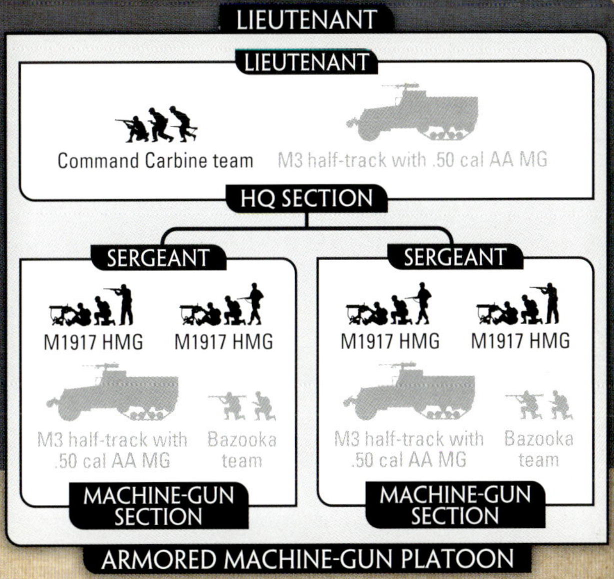

ARMORED ASSAULT GUN PLATOON

PLATOON

3 M8 Scott HMC	120 points
2 M8 Scott HMC	80 points

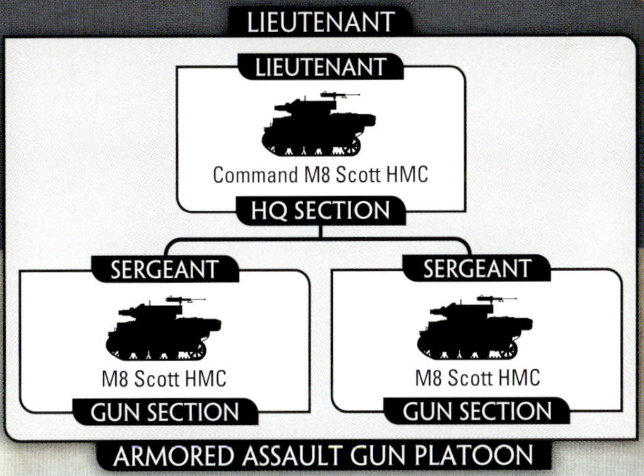

M8 SCOTT HMC

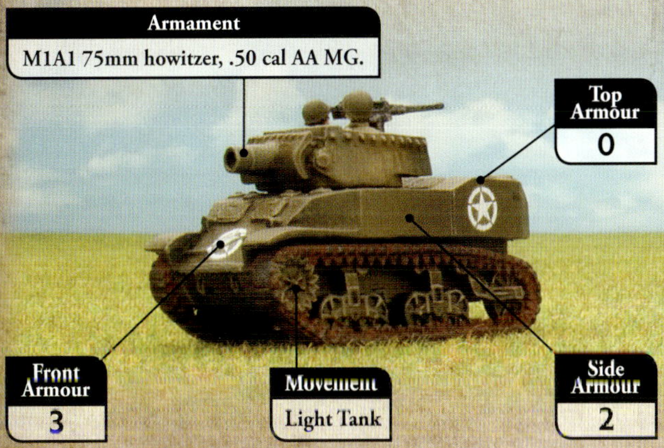

Weapon	Range	ROF	AT	FP	Notes
M1A1 75mm howitzer	16"/40cm	2	6	3+	Smoke.
Firing bombardments	64"/160cm	-	3	6	

RIFLE COMPANY

RELUCTANT | CONSCRIPT
CONFIDENT | TRAINED
FEARLESS | VETERAN

INFANTRY COMPANY

HEADQUARTERS

HEADQUARTERS
- Company Command Carbine team
- 2iC Command Carbine team
- Bazooka team
- Bazooka team

Rifle Company HQ

Headquarters

Company HQ	10 points

Options

- Add Bazooka teams for +15 points per team.
- Add up to three Sniper teams for +50 points per team.

COMBAT PLATOONS

- INFANTRY — Rifle Platoon (23)
- INFANTRY — Rifle Platoon (23)
- INFANTRY — Rifle Platoon (23)
- INFANTRY — Weapons Platoon (24)

WEAPONS PLATOONS

- MACHINE-GUNS — Machine-gun Platoon (24)
- MACHINE-GUNS — Machine-gun Platoon (24)
- ARTILLERY — Mortar Platoon (25)
- ANTI-TANK — Anti-tank Platoon (25)

REGIMENTAL SUPPORT PLATOONS

- ANTI-TANK — Anti-tank Platoon (25)

DIVISIONAL SUPPORT PLATOONS

- ARMOUR — Tank Platoon (15); Light Tank Platoon (17)
- ARMOUR — Tank Destroyer Platoon (27); Towed Tank Destroyer Platoon (27)
- RECONNAISSANCE — Cavalry Recon Platoon (26)
- ARTILLERY — Field Artillery Battery (28)
- ARTILLERY — Field Artillery Battery (28); Anti-aircraft Artillery (Self-propelled) Platoon (29)
- ARTILLERY — Field Artillery Battery (28); Field Artillery Battery (155mm) (29); Armoured Field Artillery Battery (28)
- AIRCRAFT — Air Support (26)

The Truscott Trot

Long-distance speed marches were a major feature of an infantryman's training. Some officers, like General Truscott of the 3rd Infantry Division, trained their troops so hard that they dubbed speed marching the 'Truscott Trot'.

All this practice paid off during Patton's drive to Palermo in the Sicily campaign. The men of the 3rd Infantry Division marching on foot were able to keep pace with the neighbouring 2nd Armored Division!

In *Flames Of War* US Infantry and Man-packed Gun teams move 16"/40cm instead of the normal 12"/30cm when moving At the Double. (See page 239 of the *Flames Of War* rulebook).

COMBAT PLATOONS

RIFLE PLATOON

PLATOON

HQ Section with:

3 Rifle Squads	155 points
2 Rifle Squads	110 points

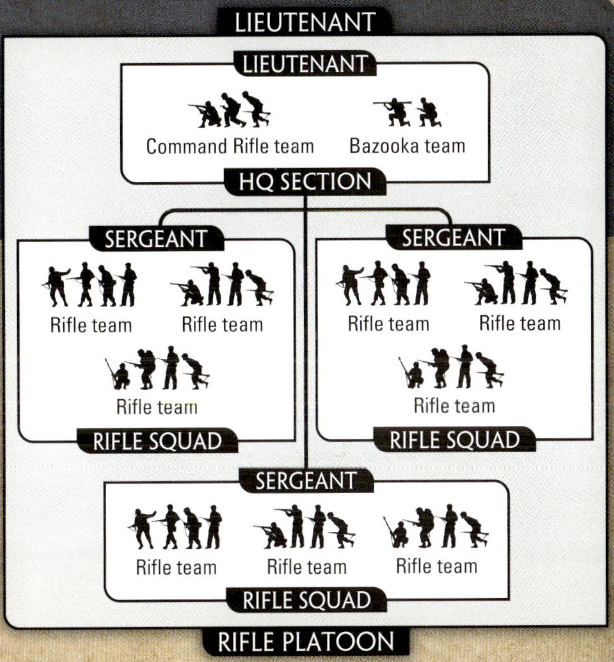

The riflemen are the foundation of the US Army. Without the rifle companies slogging their way forward, step by step, all the way to Berlin, the war will never be won. They lack the glamour of the tankers and armoured infantry, but hunkered down they can hold with the best. A rifle company can mass the greatest concentration of firepower of any force in the world. Plentiful and effective artillery with no shortage of anti-tank and tank support puts them in a class of their own.

The core of the rifle platoon is the GI armed with an M1 Garand Semi-automatic rifle, backed up by the Browning Automatic Rifle (BAR). Their automatic weapons allow them to put down an immense volume of fire, especially at short ranges, making them particularly adept at fire and manoeuvre.

US WEAPON FIREPOWER

Weapon	Volume of fire and Range (0m–500m)	Weight	Rate of Fire	Magazine	Range
M1 Carbine		5lb/2.25kg	80 rpm	Box (15)	200m
Browning Automatic Rifle (BAR)		22lb/10kg	550 rpm	Box (20)	500m
M1 Garand Rifle		9.5lb/4.3kg	80 rpm	Clip (8)	500m
Colt M1911A1 Pistol		2.5lb/1.1kg	25 rpm	Box (7)	50m
M1A1 Bazooka		12.75lb/5.8kg	4 rpm	3.5lb/1.59kg per round	100m

WEAPONS PLATOON

PLATOON

HQ and Mortar Sections with:

4 M1919	120 points
2 M1919	90 points

OPTION

- Add Jeep with .50 cal AA MG for +5 points.

Weapons Platoons may make Combat Attachments to Combat Platoons (see page 260 of the rulebook).

WEAPONS PLATOONS

MACHINE-GUN PLATOON

PLATOON

HQ Section with:

4 M1917	100 points
2 M1917	50 points

OPTIONS

- Add one Bazooka team per Machine-gun Section for +15 points per team.
- Add Jeep with .50 cal AA MG and Jeeps with trailers for +10 points for the platoon.

Machine-gun Platoons may make Combat Attachments to Combat Platoons (see page 260 of the rulebook).

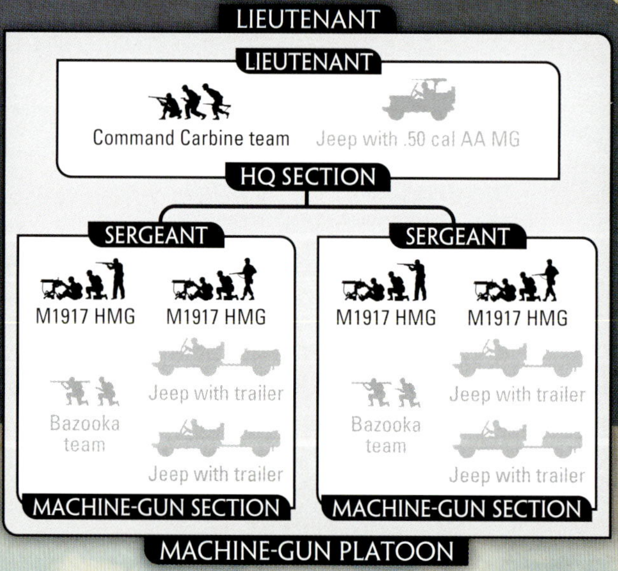

M1 81MM MORTAR

Weapon	Range	ROF	AT	FP
M1 81mm mortar	*24"/60cm*	*2*	*2*	*3+*
Firing bombardments	*40"/100cm*	*-*	*2*	*6*

M1917 HMG

Weapon	Range	ROF	AT	FP
M1917 HMG	*24"/60cm*	*6*	*2*	*6*

MORTAR PLATOON

PLATOON

HQ Section with:

6 M1 81mm	120 points
4 M1 81mm	85 points
2 M1 81mm	45 points

OPTIONS

- Add one Bazooka team per Mortar Section for +15 points per team.
- Add Jeep with .50 cal AA MG and Jeeps with trailers for +10 points for the platoon.

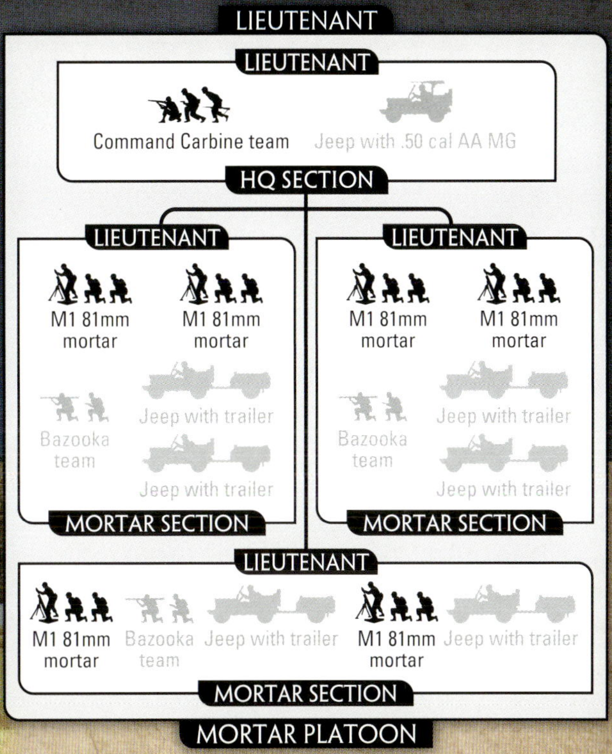

ANTI-TANK PLATOON

PLATOON

HQ Section with:

3 M1 57mm	70 points
2 M1 57mm	45 points

OPTIONS

- Add one Bazooka team per Gun Section for +15 points per team.
- Add Jeep with .50 cal AA MG and 1½-ton trucks to the platoon for +10 points for the platoon.

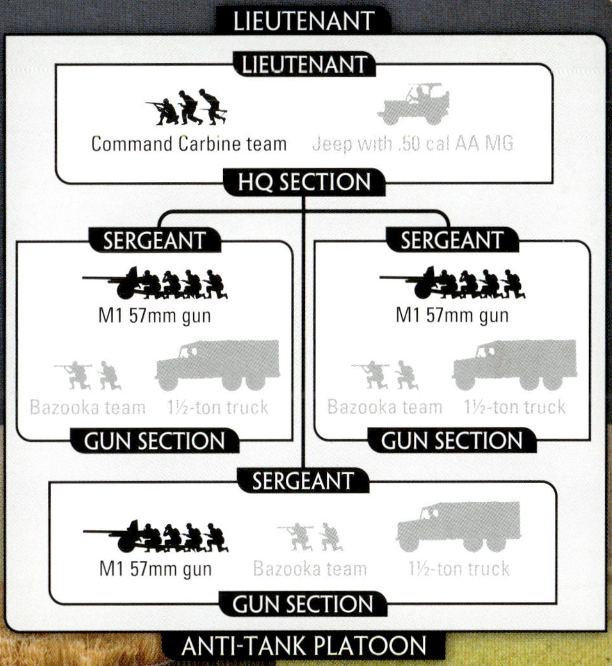

DIVISIONAL SUPPORT

RELUCTANT	CONSCRIPT
CONFIDENT	**TRAINED**
FEARLESS	VETERAN

Air Support

Priority Air Support

P-47 Thunderbolt	190 points

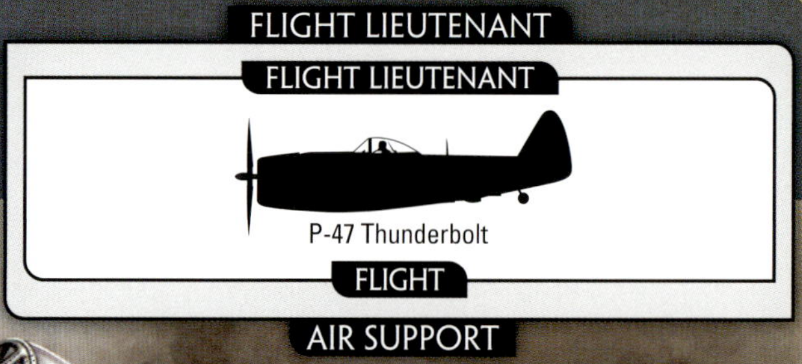

Cavalry Recon Platoon

Platoon

3 Cavalry Recon Patrols with:

3 M8 armoured cars, 3 Mortar Jeeps & 3 Recon Jeeps	210 points

2 Cavalry Recon Patrols with:

2 M8 armoured cars, 2 Mortar Jeeps & 2 Recon Jeeps	140 points

1 Cavalry Recon Patrol with:

1 M8 armoured car, 1 Mortar Jeep & 1 Recon Jeep	70 points

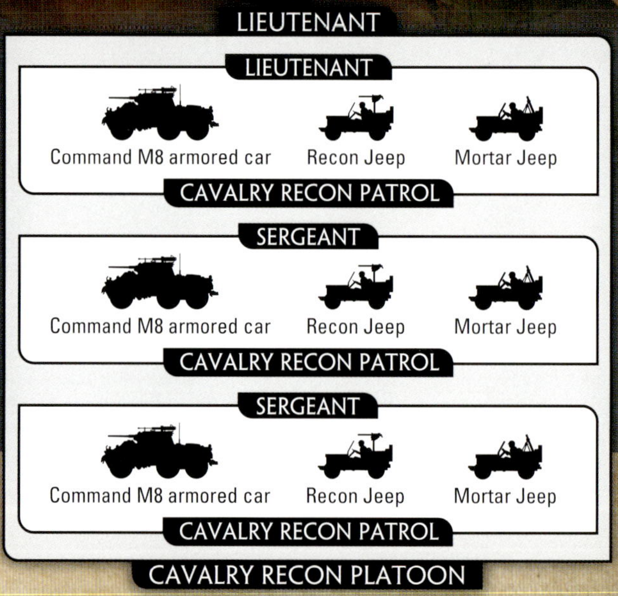

Cavalry Recon Patrols of a Cavalry Recon Platoon operate as separate platoons, each with their own command team.

Cavalry Recon Platoons are Reconnaissance Platoons (see pages 193 to 195 of the rulebook).

M8 Armored Car

Weapon	Range	ROF	AT	FP	Notes
M6 37mm gun	24"/60cm	2	7	4+	

Recon Jeep

Weapon	Range	ROF	AT	FP	Notes
AA MG	16"/40cm	3	2	6	

Towed Tank Destroyer Platoon

Platoon

Security Section and Tank Destroyer Section with:

4 M5 3in	200 points
2 M5 3in	125 points

Options

- Add up to one Bazooka team per gun for +15 points per team.
- Add M3 half-tracks with .50 cal AA MG for +5 points per half-track.

Towed Tank Destroyer Platoons use the US Tank Destroyers special rules on page 238 of the rulebook.

Towed Tank Destroyer Platoons are Reconnaissance Platoons (see pages 193 to 195 of the rulebook).

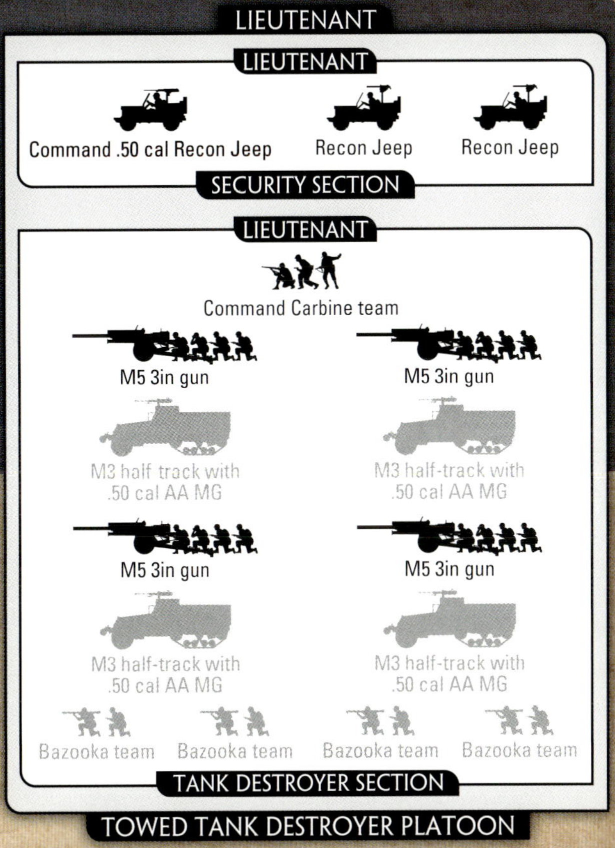

Tank Destroyer Platoon

Platoon

Security Section and Tank Destroyer Section with:

4 M10 3in GMC	320 points
2 M10 3in GMC	200 points

Tank Destroyer Platoons use the US Tank Destroyers special rules on page 238 of the rulebook.

Tank Destroyer Platoons are Reconnaissance Platoons (see pages 193 to 195 of the rulebook).

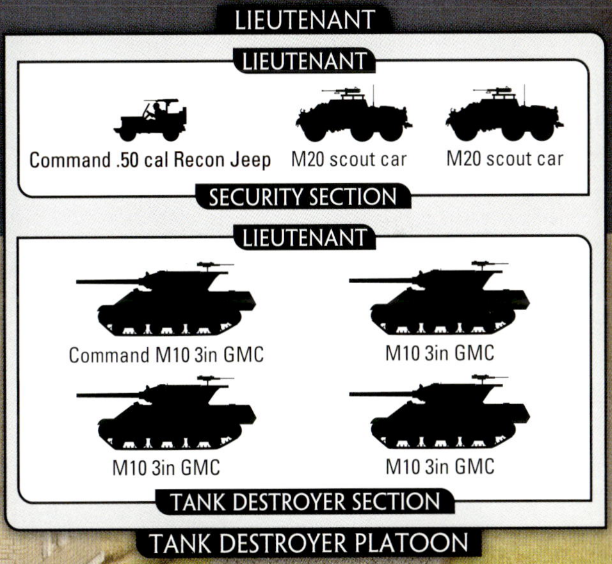

Tank destroyer platoons just deploy their Security Section at the start of the game.

Then at the start of any turn, the Tank Destroyer Section can replace the Security Section. The Security Section is then removed.

Tank destroyers must be placed at least 4"/10cm from the enemy they are Concealed from, or at least 16"/40cm away from the enemy that they are not Concealed from. Once revealed, the tank destroyers surprise the enemy with deadly fire.

Field Artillery Battery

Platoon

HQ Section with:

4 M2A1 105mm	140 points
2 M2A1 105mm	75 points

Option

- Add ¾-ton and 2½-ton trucks to the battery for +5 points.

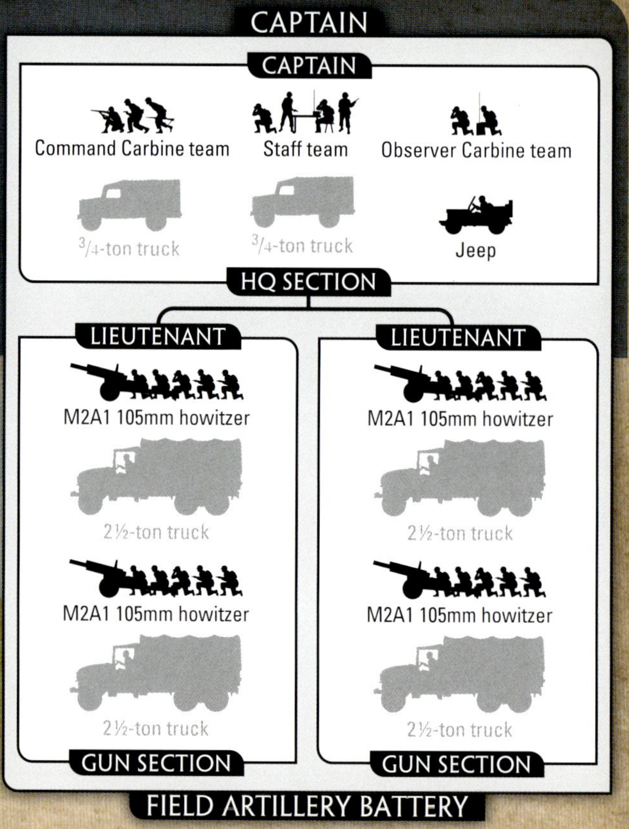

M2A1 105mm Howitzer

Notes: Breakthrough gun, Smoke bombardment

Movement: Immobile

Equipment: Gun shield, Smoke

Weapon	Range	ROF	AT	FP
M2A1 105mm howitzer	*24"/60cm*	*1*	*9*	*2+*
Firing bombardments	*72"/180cm*	*-*	*4*	*4+*

Armored Field Artillery Battery

Platoon

HQ Section with:

6 M7 Priest HMC	300 points
3 M7 Priest HMC	170 points

Options

- Add Jeep and M2 half-track for +5 points.
- Replace Jeep with M2 half-track with an AA MG for +5 points.

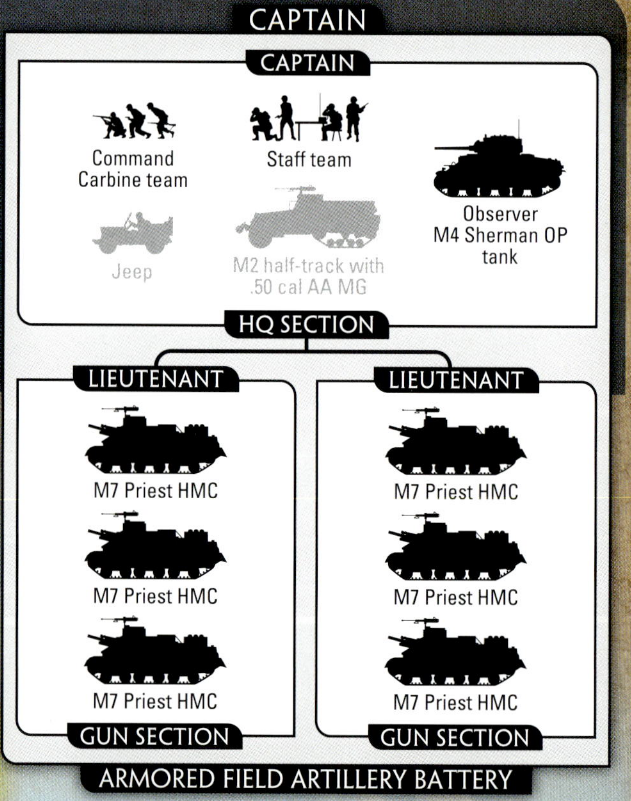

M7 Priest HMC

Armament: M2A1 105mm howitzer, .50 cal AA MG

Top Armour: 0

Front Armour: 1

Movement: Standard Tank

Side Armour: 0

Weapon	Range	ROF	AT	FP	Notes
M2A1 105mm howitzer	*24"/60cm*	*1*	*9*	*2+*	*Breakthrough gun, Hull mounted, Smoke.*
Firing bombardments	*72"/180cm*	*-*	*4*	*4+*	*Smoke bombardment.*

Field Artillery Battery (155mm)

Platoon

HQ Section with:

4 M1 155mm	210 points
2 M1 155mm	110 points

Option

- Add ¾-ton trucks and M5 high-speed tractors to the battery for +5 points.

You may not field a Field Artillery Battery (155mm) unless you are also fielding a Field Artillery Battery with at least as many guns.

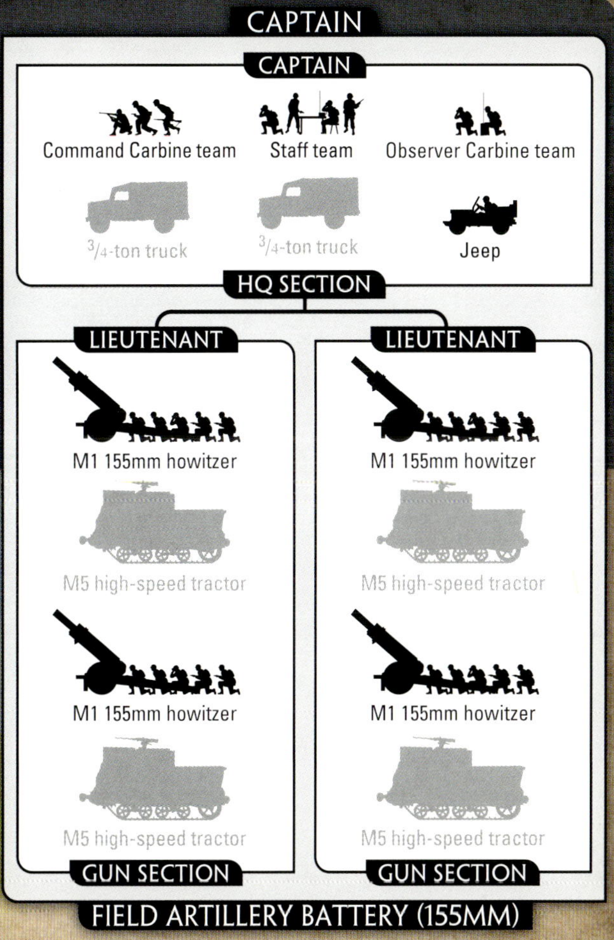

M1 155mm Howitzer

Equipment: Gun shield, Smoke

Notes: Bunker buster, Smoke bombardment

Movement: Immobile

Weapon	Range	ROF	AT	FP
M1 155mm howitzer	24"/60cm	1	10	1+
Firing bombardments	88"/220cm	-	5	2+

Anti-aircraft Artillery (Self-propelled) Platoon

Platoon

2 M15 CGMC (37mm) & 2 M16 MGMC (Quad .50 cal)	160 points
1 M15 CGMC (37mm) & 1 M16 MGMC (Quad .50 cal)	80 points

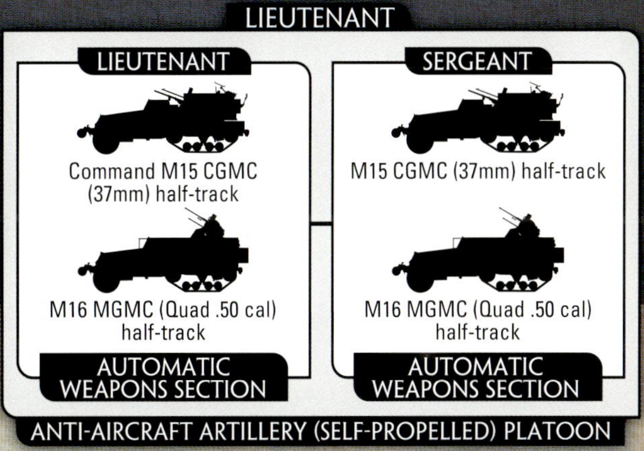

M15 CGMC (37mm) Half-track

Armament: M15 37mm combination mount with a 37mm and two .50 cal MGs

Top Armour: 0

Front Armour: 1

Movement: Wheeled

Side Armour: 0

Weapon	Range	ROF	AT	FP	Notes
M15 37mm combination mount	24"/60cm	4	5	4+	Anti-aircraft

M16 MGMC (Quad .50 cal) Half-track

Top Armour: 0

Armament: M45 quad .50 cal

Side Armour: 0

Movement: Half-tracked

Front Armour: 1

Weapon	Range	ROF	AT	FP	Notes
M45 quad .50 cal gun	16"/40cm	6	4	5+	Anti-aircraft

US ARSENAL

TANK TEAMS

Name *Weapon*	Mobility *Range*	Front *ROF*	Armour Side *Anti-tank*	Top *Firepower*	Equipment and Notes
TANKS					
M5A1 Stuart	Light Tank	4	2	1	Co-ax MG, Hull MG, AA MG.
M6 37mm gun	*24"/60cm*	*2*	*7*	*4+*	*Stabiliser.*
M4A1 Sherman	Standard Tank	6	4	1	Co-ax MG, Hull MG, .50 cal AA MG.
M3 75mm gun	*32"/80cm*	*2*	*10*	*3+*	*Smoke, Stabiliser.*
M4A1 (76mm) Sherman	Standard Tank	7	4	1	Co-ax MG, Hull MG, .50 cal AA MG, Protected ammo.
M1 76mm gun	*32"/80cm*	*2*	*12*	*3+*	*Stabiliser.*
SUPPORT WEAPONS					
M4 81mm MMC half-track	Half-tracked	1	0	0	
M1 81mm mortar	*24"/60cm*	*2*	*2*	*3+*	*Hull mounted, Minimum range 8"/20cm, Portee, Smoke.*
Firing bombardments	*40"/100cm*	*-*	*2*	*6*	*Smoke bombardment.*
M8 Scott HMC	Light Tank	3	2	0	.50 cal AA MG.
M1A1 75mm howitzer	*16"/40cm*	*2*	*6*	*3+*	*Smoke.*
Firing bombardments	*64"/160cm*	*-*	*3*	*6*	
M4 (105mm) Sherman	Standard Tank	7	4	1	Co-ax MG, Hull MG, .50 cal AA MG, Protected ammo.
M4 105mm howitzer	*24"/60cm*	*1*	*9*	*2+*	*Breakthrough gun, Slow traverse, Smoke.*
Firing bombardments	*48"/120cm*	*-*	*4*	*4+*	
TANK DESTROYERS					
M10 3in GMC	Standard Tank	4	2	0	.50 cal AA MG.
M7 3in gun	*32"/80cm*	*2*	*12*	*3+*	*Slow traverse.*
ARMORED ARTILLERY					
M7 Priest HMC	Standard Tank	1	0	0	.50 cal AA MG.
M2A1 105mm howitzer	*24"/60cm*	*1*	*9*	*2+*	*Breakthrough gun, Hull mounted, Smoke.*
Firing bombardments	*72"/180cm*	*-*	*4*	*4+*	*Smoke bombardment.*
M4A1 Sherman OP	Standard Tank	6	4	1	Co-ax MG, Hull MG, .50 cal AA MG.
M3 75mm gun	*32"/80cm*	*1*	*10*	*3+*	*Smoke.*
ANTI-AIRCRAFT					
M16 MGMC (Quad .50 cal)	Half-tracked	1	0	0	
M45 quad .50 cal gun	*16"/40cm*	*6*	*4*	*5+*	*Anti-aircraft*
M15 CGMC (37mm)	Wheeled	1	0	0	
M15 37mm combination mount	*24"/60cm*	*4*	*5*	*4+*	*Anti-aircraft*
RECONNAISSANCE					
M8 armored car	Wheeled	1	0	0	Co-ax MG, .50 cal AA MG.
M6 37mm gun	*24"/60cm*	*2*	*7*	*4+*	
Mortar Jeep	Jeep	-	-	-	
M2 60mm mortar	*24"/60cm*	*2*	*1*	*3+*	*Can fire over friendly troops.*
Firing bombardments	*32"/80cm*	*-*	*1*	*6*	
Recon Jeep	Jeep	-	-	-	
AA MG	*16"/40cm*	*3*	*2*	*6*	
.50 cal Recon Jeep	Jeep	-	-	-	
.50 cal AA MG	*16"/40cm*	*3*	*4*	*5+*	
M20 scout car	Jeep	1	0	0	
.50 cal AA MG	*16"/40cm*	*3*	*4*	*5+*	
VEHICLE MACHINE-GUNS					
Vehicle MG	*16"/40cm*	*3*	*2*	*6*	*ROF 1 if other weapons fire.*
.50 cal Vehicle MG	*16"/40cm*	*3*	*4*	*5+*	*ROF 1 if other weapons fire.*

Gun Teams

Weapon	Mobility	Range	ROF	Anti-tank	Firepower	Notes
M2 .50 cal MG	Man-packed	16"/40cm	3	4	5+	
M1919 LMG team	Man-packed	16"/40cm	5	2	6	ROF 2 when pinned down or moving.
M1917 HMG team	Man-packed	24"/60cm	6	2	6	ROF 3 when pinned down or moving.
M2 60mm mortar	Man-packed	24"/60cm	2	1	3+	Minimum range 8"/20cm.
Firing bombardments		32"/80cm	-	1	6	
M1 81mm mortar	Man-packed	24"/60cm	2	2	3+	Smoke, Minimum range 8"/20cm.
Firing bombardments		40"/100cm	-	2	6	Smoke bombardment.
M3 37mm gun	Light	24"/60cm	3	7	4+	Gun shield.
M1 57mm gun	Medium	24"/60cm	3	10	4+	Gun shield, No HE.
M5 3in gun	Immobile	32"/80cm	2	12	3+	Gun shield.
M2A1 105mm howitzer	Immobile	24"/60cm	1	9	2+	Breakthrough gun, Gun shield, Smoke.
Firing bombardments		72"/180cm	-	4	4+	Smoke bombardment.
M1 155mm howitzer	Immobile	24"/60cm	1	10	1+	Bunker buster, Gun shield, Smoke.
Firing bombardments		88"/220cm	-	5	2+	Smoke bombardment.

Infantry Teams

Team	Range	ROF	Anti-tank	Firepower	Notes
Carbine team	8"/20cm	1	1	6	Automatic rifles.
SMG team	16"/40cm	3	1	6	Full ROF when moving.
Rifle team	16"/40cm	1	2	6	Automatic rifles.
Rifle/MG team	16"/40cm	2	2	6	
Bazooka team	8"/20cm	1	10	5+	Tank assault 4.
Observer Carbine team	8"/20cm	1	1	6	Automatic rifles, Observer.
Staff team			cannot shoot		Moves as a Heavy Gun team.

Transport Teams

Vehicle	Mobility	Armour Front	Armour Side	Armour Top	Equipment and Notes
Trucks					
Jeep or Jeep with trailer	Jeep	-	-	-	Optional Passenger-fired AA MG or .50 cal AA MG.
Dodge ¾-ton 1½-ton truck	Wheeled	-	-	-	
GMC 2½-ton truck	Wheeled	-	-	-	
M5 high-speed tractor	Standard Tank	-	-	-	.50 cal AA MG
Armoured Personnel Carriers					
M2 or M3 half-track	Half-tracked	1	0	0	Optional Passenger-fired AA MG or .50 cal AA MG.

Aircraft

Aircraft	Weapon	To Hit	Anti-tank	Firepower	Notes
P-47 Thunderbolt	MG	2+	6	5+	
	Bombs	4+	5	1+	

The modern army commander must free himself from routine methods and show a comprehensive grip of technical matters, for he must be in a position continually to adapt his ideas of warfare to the facts and possibilities of the moment.

—Generalfeldmarshall Erwin Rommel

You may be seated.

What excellent specimens of Aryan manhood I see before me here today. No doubt you are all eager to begin your training so I shall not keep you long. It is my custom to provide a little talk to all our new recruits.

Have you seen the latest issue of Signal? Yes? Good, well perhaps you noticed, under the piece on 'Victory in the East', this excellent editorial. If you will permit me:

'Like a phoenix ascendant, Germany is rising once again from the false defeat contrived by our traitorous leaders in the First World War. The Treaty of Versailles was foisted upon an undefeated army and a nation willing to do anything to achieve victory. Under the glorious leadership of our beloved Führer, Germany is reclaiming its rightful place at the head of nations.'

We must all be willing to do anything, anything to have the Fatherland rule the world!

So today I'd like to expand upon this editorial for you the newest men to be given the honour of wearing the uniform of a German soldier.

The reviled Treaty attempted to limit the strength of the German armed forces. This proud martial nation was expected to make do with an army of only 100,000 men.

Ha! But they could not hold us down for long. Little did the smug French and British suspect that the German army under the inspired command of General von Seeckt, would begin training for the new age of mechanised warfare in secret. I can recall our first manoeuvres—conducted using cars with cardboard cutouts as tanks, and wooden barrels as anti-tank guns. Yes, you may well laugh but such exercises displayed the ingenuity and determination of the German soldier.

Our indignant Führer soon tore up the Treaty and rearmament began in earnest. Our rapidly expanding defence force—the Wehrmacht—under the guidance of such visionary commanders as Guderian and Nehring, pioneered a new type of warfare, one that would shock the world—Blitzkrieg—lightning war.

You men will quickly come to appreciate the effectiveness of this revolutionary method of attack before which nothing can stand. As soldiers of the mighty German Wehrmacht each of you will have to carry your part of the attack. What part you shall be given we shall see, but remember—each part is vital to the whole.

Like a bolt from the heavens the Fallschirmjäger, our daring paratroopers, drop from the sky upon the unsuspecting enemy. They capture key defensive positions behind the

front line that could threaten our attack and seize important bridges to speed the advance of our unstoppable Panzers.

Next, the Panzergrenadiers, our hard-fighting mounted infantry, launch their attack supported by the excellent guns of the German artillery—the envy of the world for their marvellous engineering. Simultaneously, our dreaded dive-bomber—the Stuka—comes screaming from the sky to unleash its deadly load upon the disintegrating enemy defences. The ill-prepared enemy cannot hope to resist such a concentration of strength and inevitably a breach is torn in the front line.

Now, the signal is given and the Panzer divisions roll forward. These mighty machines, yet another example of the superiority of German engineering, are the armoured spearhead of the Wehrmacht. The tanks smash through the shattered defenders. They drive deep into the enemy rear, the speed of their advance spreading confusion and panic. The enemy command is paralysed.

Back at the shattered front line, the Grenadiers, men inured to hardship by the rigours of the march, move forward to relieve their mounted brethren. While the 'hard as bone' Grenadiers roll up the remnants of the enemy front line, the Panzergrenadiers leap aboard their famous half-tracks. They push through the ever-widening breach in the enemy lines to exploit the shock and disorder spread by the marauding Panzers.

Our guileless enemies have no answer to this devastating combined arms attack. They cannot hope to match the skill and initiative of the German soldier on the battlefield.

Let me gaze into the eyes of the men our beloved Führer has chosen to restore Greater Germany to pre-eminence in Europe. Do you have the spirit necessary? The will to crush underfoot the weak and corrupt democracies that rot while Bolsheviks scheme to enslave the peoples of Europe. All who oppose us must be eliminated! There is no room for traitors to the cause. We are the saviours of a new Europe united under our banners, champions of a new age. You lucky men will partake in this glorious crusade, like your ancestors the Teutonic Knights who swept through the eastern lands. Onward for the Fatherland and the 'Thousand Year Reich'!

Panzerkompanie

(ARMOURED COMPANY)

HEER	
RELUCTANT	CONSCRIPT
CONFIDENT	TRAINED
FEARLESS	**VETERAN**

SS	
RELUCTANT	CONSCRIPT
CONFIDENT	TRAINED
FEARLESS	**VETERAN**

TANK COMPANY

HEADQUARTERS

- HEADQUARTERS: Company Command tank, 2iC Command tank — Panzerkompanie HQ

HEADQUARTERS

Company HQ with:

	Heer	SS
2 Panzer IV H	180 points	200 points
2 Panther A	375 points	425 points

COMBAT PLATOONS

- ARMOUR — Panzer Platoon 35
- ARMOUR — Panzer Platoon 35
- ARMOUR — Panzer Platoon 35
- ARMOUR — Panzer Platoon 35

WEAPONS PLATOONS

- ANTI-AIRCRAFT — Panzer Anti-aircraft Gun Platoon 35

DIVISIONAL SUPPORT PLATOONS

- ARMOUR — Heavy Tank Platoon 48
- ARMOUR — Assault Gun Platoon 50; Tank-hunter Platoon 49; Panzergrenadier Anti-tank Gun Platoon 42
- INFANTRY — Gepanzerte Panzergrenadier Platoon 37; Panzergrenadier Platoon 41
- INFANTRY — Gepanzerte Panzergrenadier Platoon 37; Panzergrenadier Platoon 41
- RECONNAISSANCE — Panzerspäh Patrol 51
- ARTILLERY — Artillery Battery 52; Armoured Artillery Battery 52
- ANTI-AIRCRAFT — Heavy Anti-aircraft Gun Platoon 51
- AIRCRAFT — Air Support 48

HEER AND SS

Like the other nations the Germans' armed forces are divided in to sea, air and land. However, as well as the regular Army, or *Heer*, the Germans also have *Waffen-SS* forces fighting in their land forces.

The *Heer* holds on to many of the long and proud traditions of the old German Imperial Army and the still older Prussian Army. Many of its higher officers are career soldiers from proud aristocratic military families, while the lower level officers and the other ranks are drawn from all walks of German society.

The *Waffen-SS* are the military wing of Hitler's Nazi Party. They are made up of volunteers, initially picked for their fine Germanic bearing and political allegiance. They rapidly expanded throughout the war and produced some of the best armoured divisions of the Germans forces.

Often in the field the rivalry between the *Heer* and *Waffen-SS* was great, with one group resenting being commanded by the other. At other times they could work together like a well-oiled machine.

COMBAT PLATOONS

PANZER PLATOON

PLATOON		
5 Panzer IV H	450 points	500 points
4 Panzer IV H	360 points	400 points
3 Panzer IV H	270 points	300 points
5 Panther A	940 points	1060 points
4 Panther A	750 points	850 points
3 Panther A	560 points	640 points

You must field at least one Panzer Platoon entirely equipped with the same model of tank as the Company HQ.

The Panzerkompanie is the strike arm of the German Army. Armed with powerful Panzer IV H and Panther A tanks that are heavier, better armed and more mobile than those of your enemies. They are manned by highly experienced tank crews.

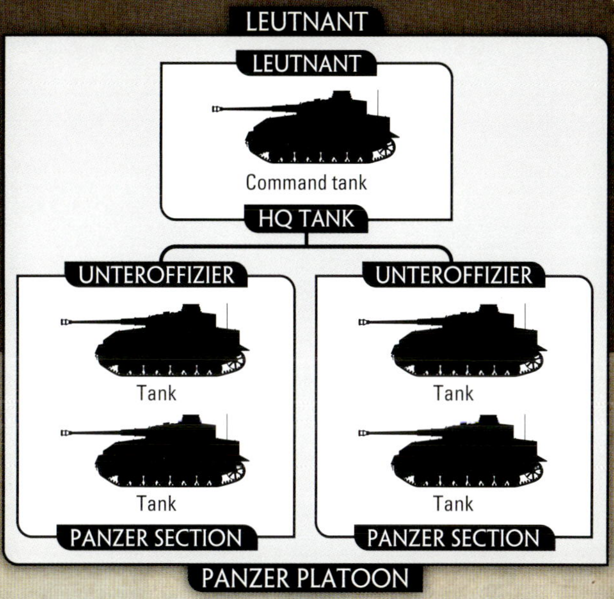

PANTHER A

Weapon	Range	ROF	AT	FP	Notes
7.5cm KwK42 gun	32"/80cm	2	14	3+	

PANZER IV H

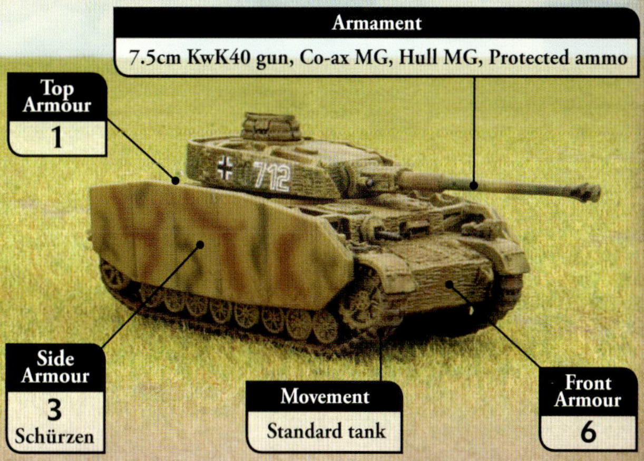

Weapon	Range	ROF	AT	FP	Notes
7.5cm KwK40 gun	32"/80cm	2	11	3+	

WEAPONS PLATOONS

PANZER ANTI-AIRCRAFT GUN PLATOON

PLATOON		
3 Sd Kfz 7/1 (Quad 2cm)	120 points	135 points
2 Sd Kfz 7/1 (Quad 2cm)	80 points	90 points
3 Armoured Sd Kfz 7/1 (Quad 2cm)	150 points	185 points
2 Armoured Sd Kfz 7/1 (Quad 2cm)	100 points	125 points

Gepanzerte Panzergrenadierkompanie

(Armoured Motorised Infantry Company)

RELUCTANT	CONSCRIPT	RELUCTANT	CONSCRIPT
CONFIDENT	TRAINED	CONFIDENT	TRAINED
FEARLESS	**VETERAN**	**FEARLESS**	**VETERAN**
HEER		SS	

MECHANISED COMPANY

HEADQUARTERS

Company Command SMG team — 2iC Command SMG team

Sd Kfz 251/1 half-track — Sd Kfz 251/1 half-track

UNTEROFFIZER: Panzerschrek team, Sd Kfz 251/1 half-track — ANTI-TANK SECTION

Gepanzerte Panzergrenadierkompanie HQ

Headquarters

	Heer	SS
Company HQ	65 points	75 points

Options

- Replace either or both Command SMG teams with Command Panzerknacker SMG teams for +5 points per team or Command Panzerfaust SMG teams for +10 points per team.
- Add an Anti-tank Section for +40 points.

The Company HQ of a Gepanzerte Panzergrenadier-kompanie may use the Mounted Assault special rule (see page 243 of the rulebook).

COMBAT PLATOONS

- INFANTRY: Gepanzerte Panzergrenadier Platoon — 37
- INFANTRY: Gepanzerte Panzergrenadier Platoon — 37
- INFANTRY: Gepanzerte Panzergrenadier Platoon — 37
- MACHINE-GUNS: Gepanzerte Heavy Platoon — 37

WEAPONS PLATOONS

- ARMOUR: Gepanzerte Cannon Platoon — 38
- ANTI-TANK: Gepanzerte Anti-tank Gun Platoon — 38
- ANTI-AIRCRAFT: Panzergrenadier Anti-aircraft Gun Platoon — 42

REGIMENTAL SUPPORT PLATOONS

- ARTILLERY: Self-propelled Infantry Gun Platoon — 39
- INFANTRY: Gepanzerte Pioneer Platoon — 39

DIVISIONAL SUPPORT PLATOONS

- ARMOUR: Panzer Platoon — 35; Heavy Tank Platoon — 48
- ARMOUR: Assault Gun Platoon — 50; Tank-hunter Platoon — 49; Panzergrenadier Anti-tank Gun Platoon — 42
- INFANTRY: Panzergrenadier Platoon — 41
- RECONNAISSANCE: Panzerspäh Patrol — 51
- ARTILLERY: Artillery Battery — 52; Armoured Artillery Battery — 52
- ANTI-AIRCRAFT: Heavy Anti-aircraft Gun Platoon — 51
- AIRCRAFT: Air Support — 48

Combat Platoons

Gepanzerte Panzergrenadier Platoon

Platoon

HQ Section with:		
3 Panzergrenadier Squads	220 points	260 points
2 Panzergrenadier Squads	155 points	190 points

Options

- Replace the Command MG team with a Command Panzerknacker SMG team for +5 points or a Command Panzerfaust SMG team for +10 points.
- Replace Sd Kfz 251/10 (3.7cm) half-track with a Sd Kfz 251/1 half-track at no cost.

Gepanzerte Panzergrenadier Platoons may use the Mounted Assault special rule (see page 243 of the rulebook).

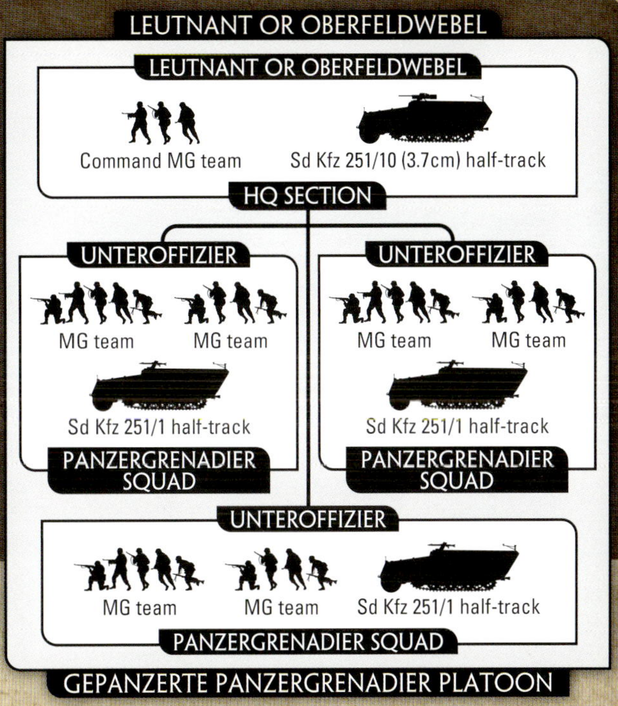

Gepanzerte Heavy Platoon

Platoon

HQ Section with:		
2 Sd Kfz 251/9 (7.5cm), 4 MG42 & 2 Sd Kfz 251/2 (8cm)	330 points	390 points
2 Sd Kfz 251/9 (7.5cm), 2 MG42 & 2 Sd Kfz 251/2 (8cm)	255 points	300 points
2 Sd Kfz 251/9 (7.5cm) & 4 MG42	245 points	290 points
2 Sd Kfz 251/9(7.5cm) & 2 MG42	170 points	200 points
4 MG42 & 2 Sd Kfz 251/2 (8cm)	250 points	300 points
2 MG42 & 2 Sd Kfz 251/2 (8cm)	175 points	210 points
4 MG42	165 points	200 points
2 MG42	90 points	110 points

Gepanzerte Heavy Platoons may make Combat Attachments to Combat Platoons (see page 260 of the rulebook).

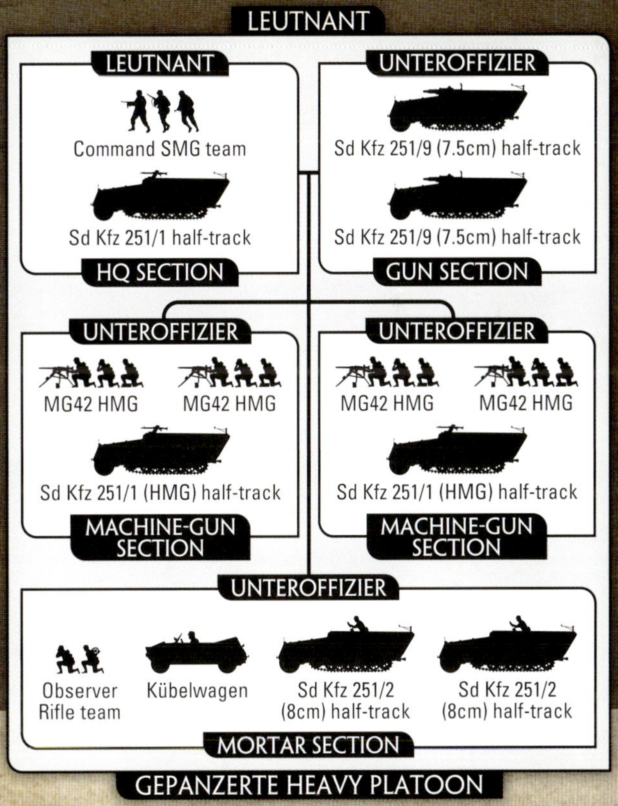

Mounted Assault

German armoured infantry units are specifically trained to fight from their half-tracks. Whereas US and British armoured infantry use their half-tracks as battle taxis to get them close to the enemy then dismount, German Gepanzerte Panzergrenadier Platoons assault light opposition still mounted in their half-tracks.

In *Flames Of War* this means you can launch an assault with your Gepanzerte Panzergrenadier Platoon while the teams are still mounted in your half-tracks. While mounted they get to fight the Assault as if they were Tank teams. They can then dismount and continue the fight on foot. See the Mounted Assault German special rule on page 243 of the *Flames Of War* rulebook.

WEAPONS PLATOONS

Gepanzerte Cannon Platoon

Platoon

6 Sd Kfz 251/9 (7.5cm)	240 points	270 points
4 Sd Kfz 251/9 (7.5cm)	160 points	180 points
2 Sd Kfz 251/9 (7.5cm)	80 points	90 points

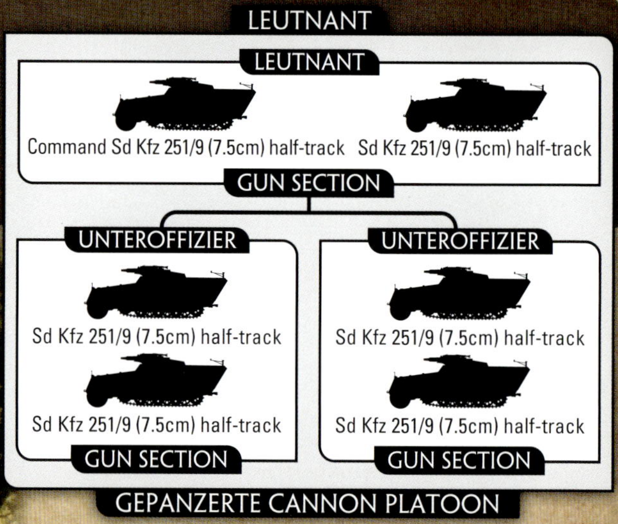

Gepanzerte Anti-tank Gun Platoon

Platoon

HQ Section with:

3 7.5cm PaK40	155 points	180 points
2 7.5cm PaK40	105 points	120 points

Option

- Add Sd Kfz 251/1 half-tracks for +10 points per half-track.

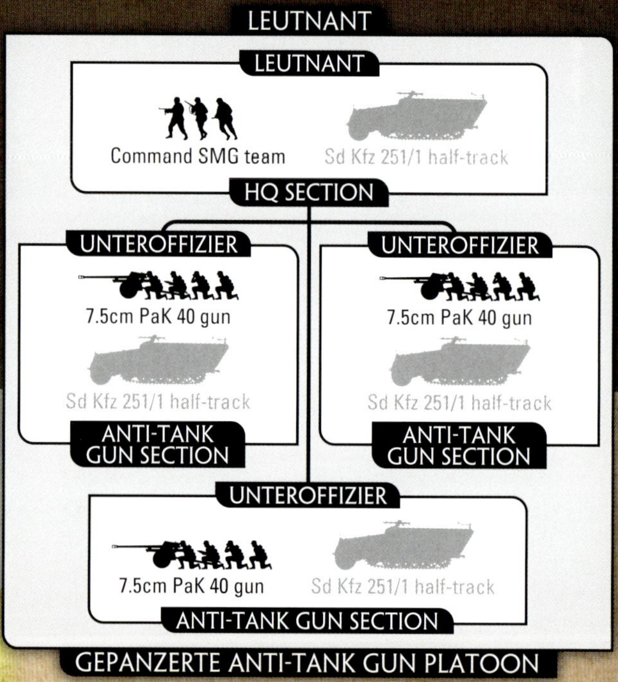

Sd Kfz 251/1

Sd Kfz 251/10 (3.7cm)

Weapon	Range	ROF	AT	FP	Notes
3.7cm PaK36 gun	16"/40cm	2	6	4+	Hull mounted

Sd Kfz 251/9 (7.5cm)

Weapon	Range	ROF	AT	FP	Notes
7.5cm KwK37 gun	24"/60cm	2	9	3+	Hull mounted

REGIMENAL SUPPORT PLATOONS

GEPANZERTE PIONEER PLATOON

PLATOON

HQ Section with:

3 Pioneer Squads	265 points	315 points
2 Pioneer Squads	190 points	230 points

OPTIONS

- Replace the Command Pioneer MG team with a Command Pioneer Panzerknacker SMG team for +5 points or a Command Pioneer Panzerfaust SMG team for +10 points.
- Add an additional Sd Kfz 251/7 half-track to each squad for +10 points per half-track.
- Add Pioneer Supply 3-ton truck for +25 points or Pioneer Supply Maultier for +30 points.

You may replace up to one Pioneer MG team per Pioneer Squad with a Flame-thrower team at the start of the game before deployment.

Gepanzerte Pioneer Platoons may use the Mounted Assault special rule (see page 243 of the rulebook).

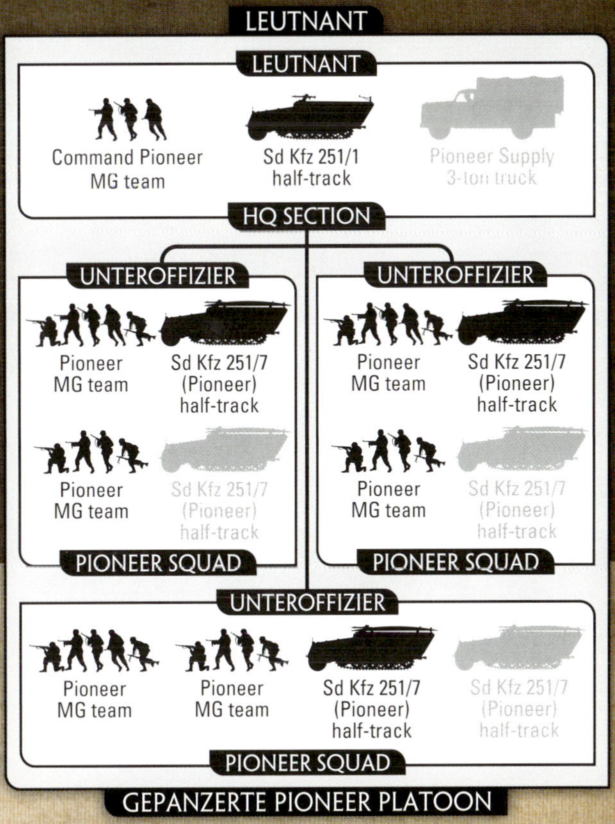

SELF-PROPELLED INFANTRY GUN PLATOON

PLATOON

HQ Section with:

2 Grille K (15cm sIG)	170 points	190 points

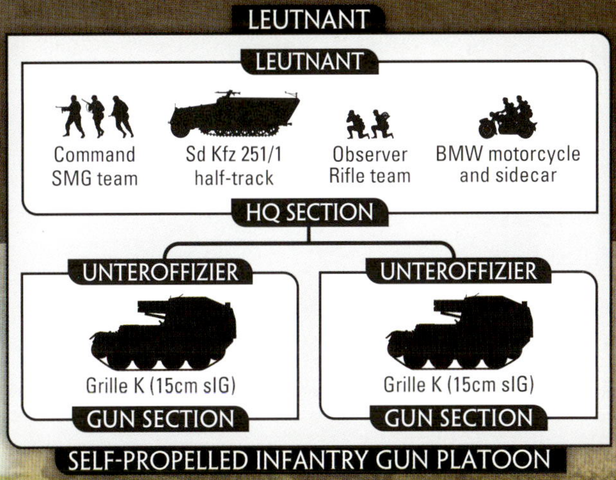

GRILLE K (15CM SIG)

Weapon	Range	ROF	AT	FP	Notes
15cm sIG33 gun	16"/40cm	1	13	1+	Bunker buster, Hull mounted
Firing bombardments	56"/140cm	-	4	2+	

Panzergrenadierkompanie

(Motorised Infantry Company)

Reluctant	Conscript
Confident	Trained
Fearless	**Veteran**

Heer

Reluctant	Conscript
Confident	Trained
Fearless	**Veteran**

SS

Mechanised Company

Headquarters

Company Command SMG team
2iC Command SMG team
Motorcycle and sidecar
Kfz 15 field car

Unteroffizier
Panzerschrek team
Kfz 70 truck
Anti-tank Section

Panzergrenadierkompanie HQ

Headquarters

	Heer	SS
Company HQ	45 points	55 points

Options

- Replace either or both Command SMG teams with Command Panzerknacker SMG teams for +5 points per team or Command Panzerfaust SMG teams for +10 points per team.
- Add an Anti-tank Section for +25 points.
- Add up to three Sniper teams for +50 points per team.

Combat Platoons

Infantry
Panzergrenadier Platoon 41

Infantry
Panzergrenadier Platoon 41

Infantry
Panzergrenadier Platoon 41

Infantry
Panzergrenadier Heavy Platoon 41

Weapons Platoons

Artillery
Panzergrenadier Infantry Gun Platoon 43

Anti-tank
Panzergrenadier Anti-tank Gun Platoon 42

Anti-aircraft
Panzergrenadier Anti-aircraft Gun Platoon 42

Regimental Support Platoons

Artillery
Self-propelled Infantry Gun Platoon 39

Infantry
Panzergrenadier Pioneer Platoon 43
Gepanzerte Pioneer Platoon 39

Divisional Support Platoons

Armour
Panzer Platoon 35
Heavy Tank Platoon 48

Armour
Assault Gun Platoon 50
Tank-hunter Platoon 49
Panzergrenadier Anti-tank Gun Platoon 42

Infantry
Gepanzerte Panzergrenadier Platoon 37

Reconnaissance
Panzerspäh Patrol 51

Artillery
Artillery Battery 52
Armoured Artillery Battery 52

Anti-aircraft
Heavy Anti-aircraft Gun Platoon 51

Aircraft
Air Support 48

COMBAT PLATOONS

PANZERGRENADIER PLATOON

PLATOON

HQ Section with:

3 Panzergrenadier Squads	185 points	225 points
2 Panzergrenadier Squads	135 points	160 points

OPTIONS

- Replace the Command MG team with a Command Panzerknacker SMG team for +5 points or a Command Panzerfaust SMG team for +10 points.

The Panzergrenadierkompanie, or motorised infantry company, forms the hard core of a Panzer or Panzergrenadier division. These motorised infantry use trucks to bring them to the battlefield. They dismount to fight on foot and are well-supported by Panzers, assault guns and mobile artillery.

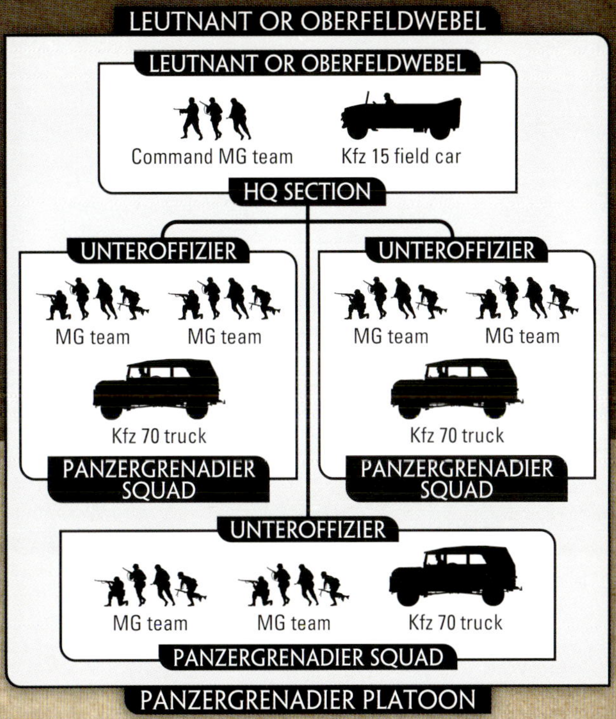

PANZERGRENADIER HEAVY PLATOON

PLATOON

HQ Section with:

4 MG42 & 2 8cm GW34	205 points	225 points
2 MG42 & 2 8cm GW34	140 points	155 points
4 MG42	140 points	155 points
2 MG42	75 points	85 points

Panzergrenadier Heavy Platoons may make Combat Attachments to Combat Platoons (see page 260 of the rulebook).

COMBAT ATTACHMENTS

Often infantry companies had additional weapons in their weapons platoons. These could be fielded as a concentrated block of firepower under their own commander, but were more often divided up among the company's platoons to add to their firepower and strength.

In *Flames Of War* you can do this with a platoon that can make Combat Attachments (see page 260 of the *Flames Of War* rulebook). The rule allows you to attach out half to all the teams from the platoon to your Combat Platoons. The attached teams become part of the Combat Platoon.

By doing this you can add additional firepower directly to your platoon as well as boosting the strength of your Combat Platoons.

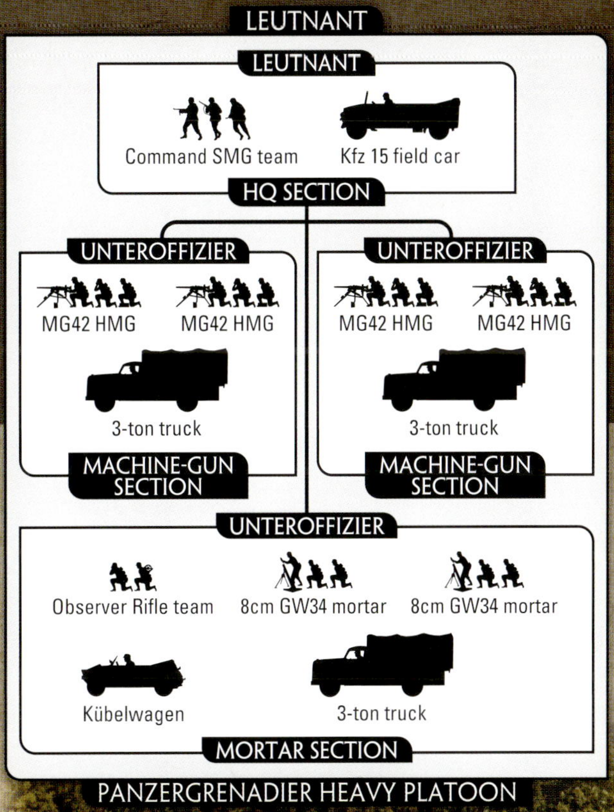

WEAPONS PLATOONS

PANZERGRENADIER ANTI-TANK GUN PLATOON

PLATOON

HQ Section with:

	Heer	SS
3 7.5cm PaK40	155 points	180 points
2 7.5cm PaK40	105 points	120 points

OPTION

- Add Kfz 15 field car and Kfz 70 trucks for +5 points for the platoon.

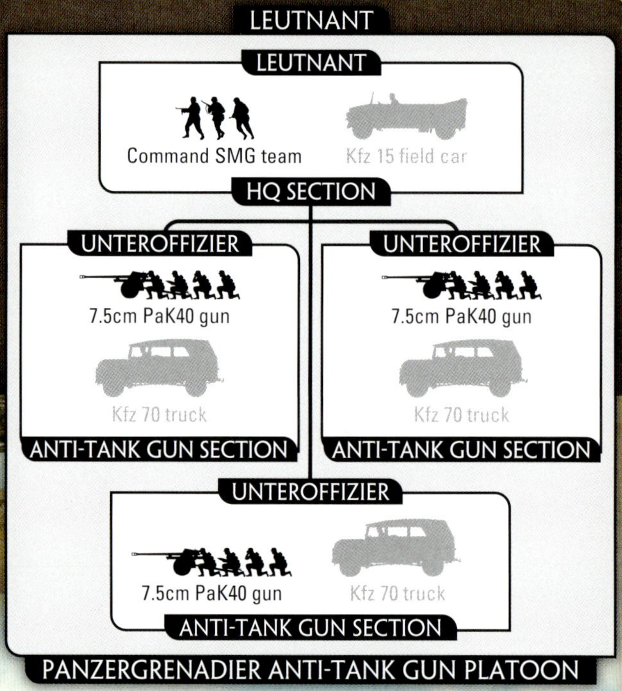

7.5CM PAK40 GUN

Weapon	Range	ROF	AT	FP
7.5cm PaK40 gun	32"/80cm	2	12	3+

PANZERGRENADIER ANTI-AIRCRAFT GUN PLATOON

PLATOON

	Heer	SS
3 Sd Kfz 10/5 (2cm)	90 points	95 points
2 Sd Kfz 10/5 (2cm)	60 points	65 points
3 Armoured Sd Kfz 10/5 (2cm)	120 points	135 points
2 Armoured Sd Kfz 10/5 (2cm)	80 points	90 points

SD KFZ 10/5 (2CM)

Weapon	Range	ROF	AT	FP	Notes
2cm FlaK38 gun	16"/40cm	4	5	5+	Anti-aircraft

ARMOURED SD KFZ 10/5 (2CM)

Weapon	Range	ROF	AT	FP	Notes
2cm FlaK38 gun	16"/40cm	4	5	5+	Anti-aircraft

Panzergrenadier Infantry Gun Platoon

Platoon

HQ Section with:

2 7.5cm leIG18	70 points	75 points

Option

- Add Kfz 15 field car and Kfz 70 trucks for +5 points for the platoon.

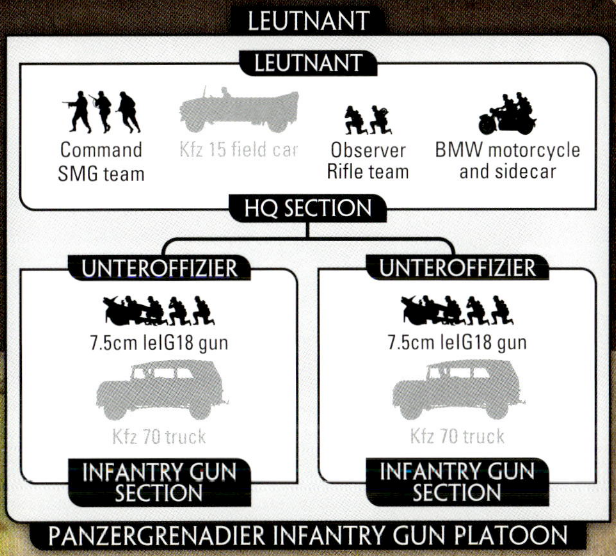

Regimental Support Platoons

Panzergrenadier Pioneer Platoon

Platoon

HQ Section with:

3 Pioneer Squads	205 points	245 points
2 Pioneer Squads	145 points	175 points

Options

- Replace Command Pioneer Rifle/MG team with Command Pioneer Panzerknacker SMG team for +5 points or Command Pioneer Panzerfaust SMG team for +10 points.
- Equip one Pioneer Rifle/MG team with a Goliath demolition carrier in addition to its normal weapons for +30 points.
- Add Pioneer Supply 3-ton truck for +25 points.

You may replace up to one Pioneer Rifle/MG team per Pioneer Squad with a Flame-thrower team at the start of the game before deployment.

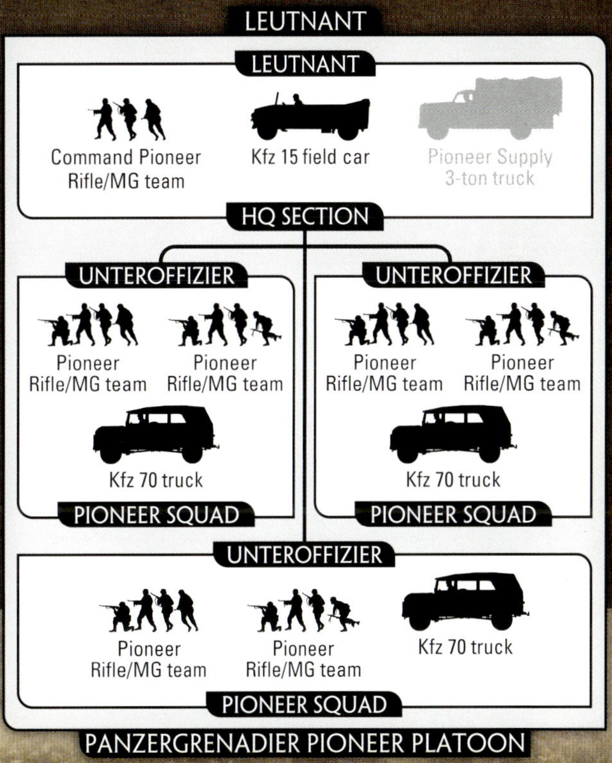

Grenadierkompanie

(INFANTRY COMPANY)

RELUCTANT | CONSCRIPT
CONFIDENT | TRAINED
FEARLESS | VETERAN

HEER

INFANTRY COMPANY

HEADQUARTERS

HEADQUARTERS

- Company Command SMG team
- 2iC Command SMG team

UNTEROFFIZIER — ANTI-TANK SECTION: Panzerschrek team

UNTEROFFIZIER — MORTAR SECTION: 8cm GW34 mortar, 8cm GW34 mortar

Grenadierkompanie HQ

HEADQUARTERS

Company HQ	45 points

OPTIONS

- Replace either or both Command SMG teams with Command Panzerknacker SMG teams for +5 points per team or Command Panzerfaust SMG teams for +10 points per team.
- Add an Anti-tank Section for +25 points.
- Add Mortar Section for +55 points.
- Add up to three Sniper teams for +50 points per team.

COMBAT PLATOONS

- INFANTRY — Grenadier Platoon 45
- INFANTRY — Grenadier Platoon 45
- INFANTRY — Grenadier Platoon 45

WEAPONS PLATOONS

- MACHINE-GUNS — Grenadier Machine-gun Platoon 45
- MACHINE-GUNS — Grenadier Machine-gun Platoon 45
- ARTILLERY — Grenadier Mortar Platoon 46

REGIMENTAL SUPPORT PLATOONS

- ARTILLERY — Grenadier Infantry Gun Platoon 46
- ANTI-TANK — Grenadier Anti-tank Gun Platoon 47
- INFANTRY — Grenadier Pioneer Platoon 47

DIVISIONAL SUPPORT PLATOONS

- ARMOUR — Panzer Platoon 35; Heavy Tank Platoon 48
- ARMOUR — Assault Gun Platoon 50; Tank-hunter Platoon 49; Panzergrenadier Anti-tank Gun Platoon 42
- ARTILLERY — Artillery Battery 52
- ANTI-AIRCRAFT — Heavy Anti-aircraft Gun Platoon 51
- AIRCRAFT — Air Support 48

COMBAT PLATOONS

GRENADIER PLATOON

PLATOON

HQ Section with:

3 Grenadier Squads	155 points
2 Grenadier Squads	110 points

OPTION

- Replace Command Rifle/MG team with a Command Panzerknacker SMG team for +5 points or Command Panzerfaust SMG team for +10 points.

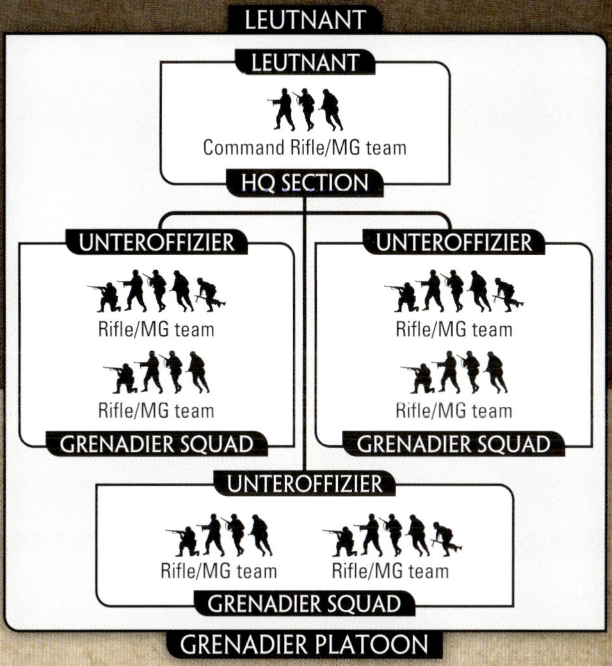

A Grenadierkompanie, or infantry company, is the finest infantry force you can command. The troops are all experienced veterans and their equipment is as good as it gets. Of course, you'll always be outnumbered, but there's nothing like the satisfaction of facing an overwhelming horde... and winning! Backed by the best weapons that the German army can provide, from StuG assault guns to the feared Tigers, your Grenadierkompanie will never be out-gunned or out classed.

WEAPONS PLATOONS

GRENADIER MACHINE-GUN PLATOON

PLATOON

HQ Section with:

4 MG42	135 points
2 MG42	70 points

Grenadier Machine-gun Platoons may make Combat Attachments to Combat Platoons (see page 260 of the rulebook).

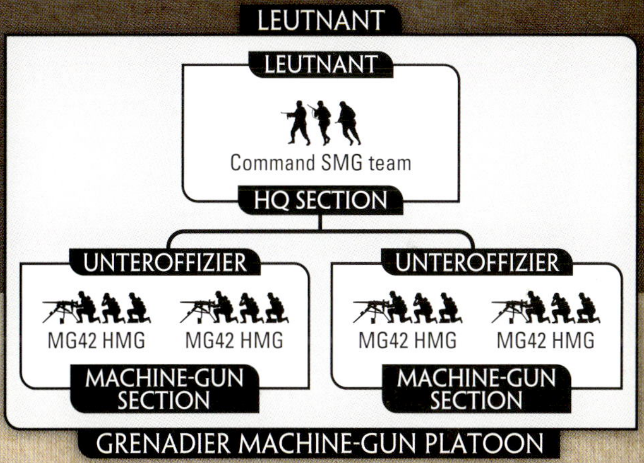

GERMAN WEAPON FIREPOWER

Weapon	Volume of fire and Range (0m – 500m)	Weight	Rate of Fire	Magazine	Range
MP40 submachine-gun		9lb/4.1kg	550 rpm	Box (32)	50m
MG42 machine-gun		25.5lb/11.6kg	1200 rpm	Belt (50)	500m
Kar98k carbine		8.6lb/3.9kg	50 rpm	Clip (5)	500m
Panzerfaust		11.5lb/5.2kg	1 shot	Single	30m

Grenadier Mortar Platoon

Platoon

HQ Section with:

6 8cm GW34	180 points
4 8cm GW34	125 points
2 8cm GW34	65 points
4 12cm sGW43	165 points
2 12cm sGW43	85 points

Option

- Add RSO tractors to 12cm sGW43 mortars for +5 points for the platoon.

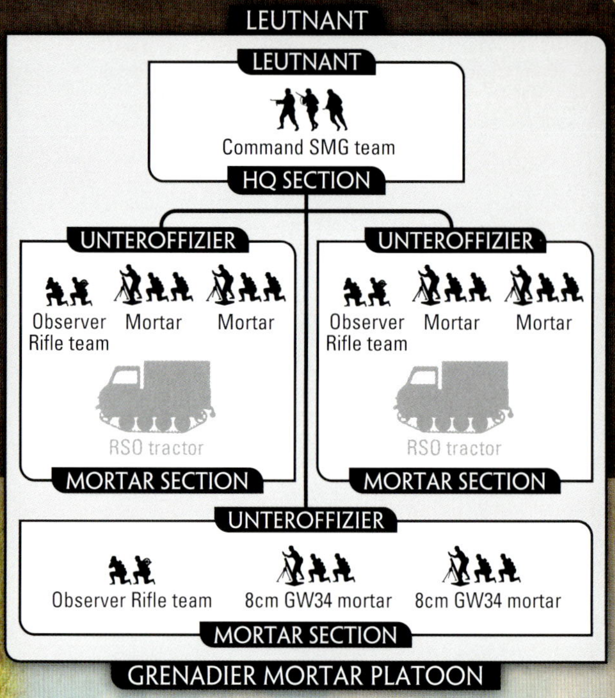

8cm GW34 Mortar

Weapon	Range	ROF	AT	FP
8cm GW34 mortar	24"/60cm	2	2	3+
Firing bombardments	40"/100cm	-	2	6

12cm sGW43 Mortar

Weapon	Range	ROF	AT	FP
12cm sGW43 mortar	56"/140cm	-	3	3+

Regimental Support Platoons

Grenadier Infantry Gun Platoon

Platoon

HQ Section with:

2 7.5cm leIG18	65 points

Options

- Replace both 7.5cm leIG18 guns with 15cm sIG33 guns for +80 points.
- Add RSO tractors for +5 points for the platoon.

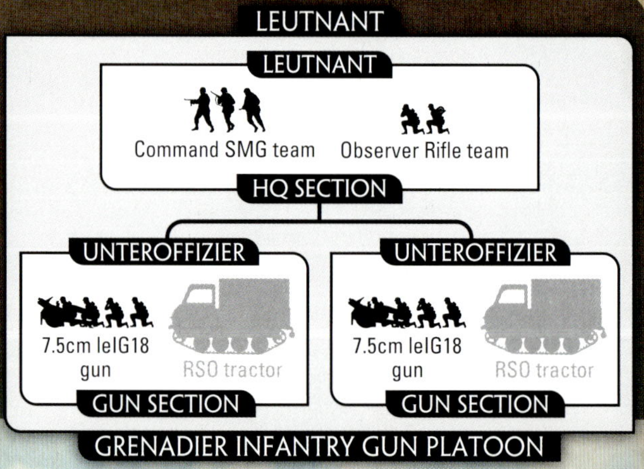

7.5cm leIG18

Weapon	Range	ROF	AT	FP
7.5cm leIG18 gun	16"/40cm	2	9	3+
Firing bombardments	48"/120cm	-	3	6

15cm sIG33

Weapon	Range	ROF	AT	FP
15cm sIG33 gun	16"/40cm	1	13	1+
Firing bombardments	56"/140cm	-	4	2+

Grenadier Anti-Tank Gun Platoon

Platoon

HQ Section with:

3 7.5cm PaK40	155 points
2 7.5cm PaK40	105 points

Option

- Add Kfz 15 field car and Kfz 70 trucks for +5 points for the platoon.

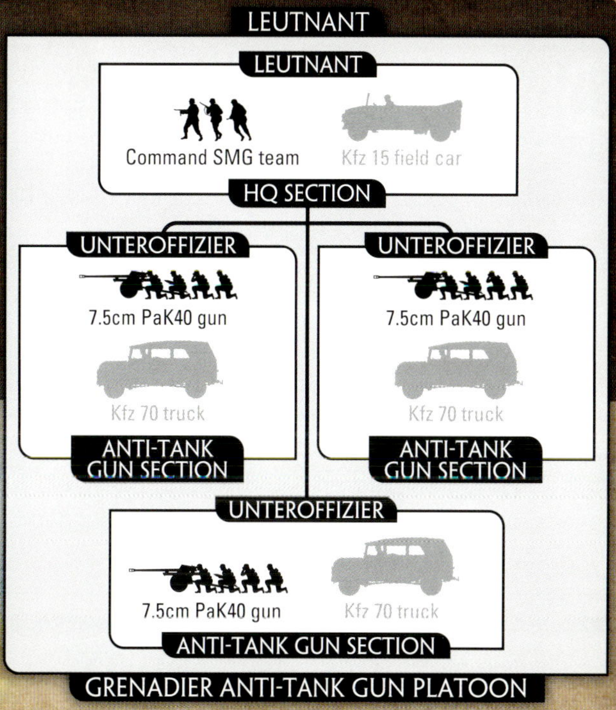

Grenadier Pioneer Platoon

Platoon

HQ Section with:

3 Pioneer Squads	235 points
2 Pioneer Squads	165 points

Options

- Replace Command Pioneer Rifle team with Command Pioneer Panzerknacker SMG team for +5 points or Command Pioneer Panzerfaust SMG team for +10 points.
- Add Pioneer Supply RSO tractor for +25 points.

You may replace up to one Pioneer Rifle team per Pioneer Squad with a Flame-thrower team at the start of the game before deployment.

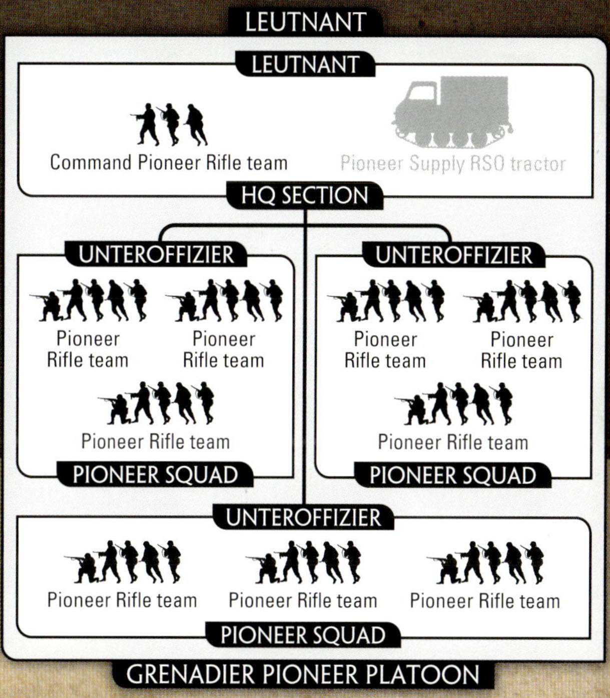

Pioneers

Pioneer is another term for combat engineer. These tough specialist troops have two combat roles. They undertake dangerous engineering assignments while under fire, like clearing and laying mines, and destroying obstacles in the way of your forces. They are also excellent assault troops, especially against fortified positions where their explosives and flame-throwers are especially useful.

In *Flames Of War* your Grenadier Pioneer Platoon gets to re-roll failed Skill tests to remove or gap fortification obstacles (see Gapping Obstacles on page 225 of the *Flames Of War* rulebook). They also re-roll failed Skill tests to hit bunkers in assaults. All your Pioneer Rifle teams have a Tank Assault 4 rating (normally teams only have Tank Assault 2), which means when they assault Tank teams they compare this with the tanks top armour rating plus its normal die roll. This makes them excellent anti-tank troops if you can catch the enemy tanks out where their defensive fire is limited.

The flame-thrower is also an important pioneer weapon. Instead of a normal to hit roll, you roll a Skill test to hit targets. Once you hit your target you automatically pin down the enemy platoon and destroy any unarmoured team hit, even those in bulletproof cover. Against bunkers they are ideal for pinning them down and leave them vulnerable to the rest of your pioneer teams. Though unlikely to knock out tanks, they can blind them and stop their defensive fire in assaults. See page 198 of the *Flames Of War* rulebook.

Divisional Support

Heer	
RELUCTANT	CONSCRIPT
CONFIDENT	TRAINED
FEARLESS	**VETERAN**

SS	
RELUCTANT	CONSCRIPT
CONFIDENT	TRAINED
FEARLESS	**VETERAN**

Air Support

Limited Air Support

Ju 87D Stuka	135 points
Ju 87G Stuka	135 points
Hs 129B	155 points

Sporadic Air Support

Ju 87D Stuka	100 points
Ju 87G Stuka	100 points
Hs 129B	115 points

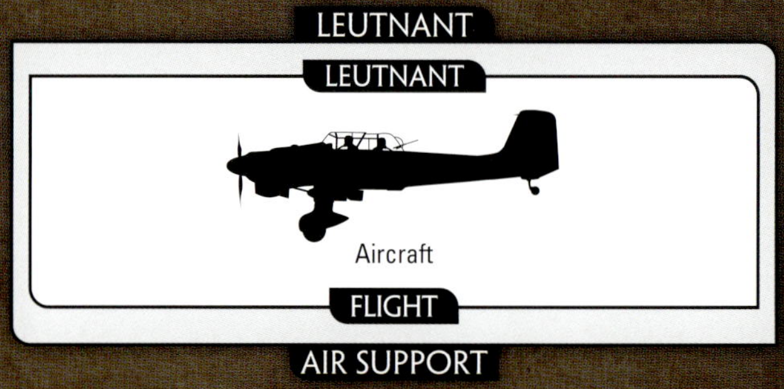

Heavy Tank Platoon

Platoon

	Heer	SS
4 Tiger I E	860 points	960 points
3 Tiger I E	645 points	720 points
2 Tiger I E	430 points	480 points
1 Tiger I E	215 points	240 points
4 Königstiger (Henschel)	1380 points	-
3 Königstiger (Henschel)	1035 points	-
2 Königstiger (Henschel)	690 points	-
1 Königstiger (Henschel)	345 points	-

A Heavy Tank Platoon uses the Tiger Aces rule (see page 244 of the rulebook). Roll for your Tiger Ace Skills before each game.

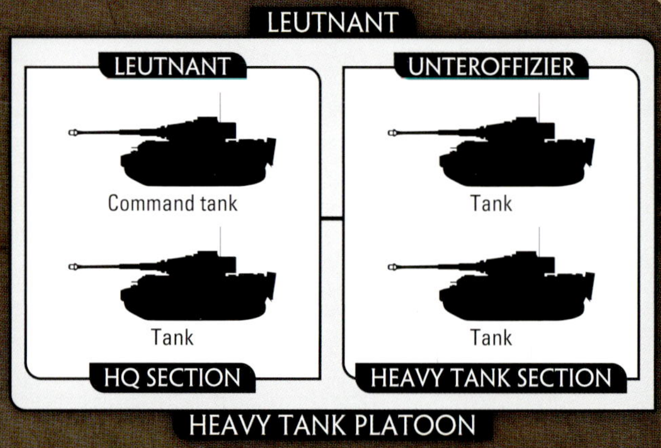

Tiger I E

Armament: 8.8cm KwK36 gun, Co-ax MG, Hull MG, Protected ammo

Top Armour: 2 | **Front Armour:** 9 | **Side Armour:** 8

Movement: Slow Tank, Wide tracks

Weapon	Range	ROF	AT	FP	Notes
8.8cm KwK36 gun	40"/100cm	2	13	3+	Slow traverse.

Königstiger (Henschel)

Armament: 8.8cm KwK43 gun, Co-ax MG, Hull MG

Top Armour: 2 | **Side Armour:** 8 | **Front Armour:** 15

Movement: Slow Tank, Overloaded

Weapon	Range	ROF	AT	FP	Notes
8.8cm KwK43 gun	40"/100cm	2	16	3+	Slow traverse.

Tank-hunter Platoon

Platoon		
4 Marder III M	255 points	285 points
3 Marder III M	190 points	215 points
2 Marder III M	125 points	145 points
4 Jagdpanzer IV	380 points	435 points
3 Jagdpanzer IV	285 points	325 points
2 Jagdpanzer IV	190 points	215 points
4 Hornisse	465 points	-
3 Hornisse	350 points	-
2 Hornisse	235 points	-
4 Jagdpanther	920 points	-
3 Jagdpanther	690 points	-
2 Jagdpanther	460 points	-

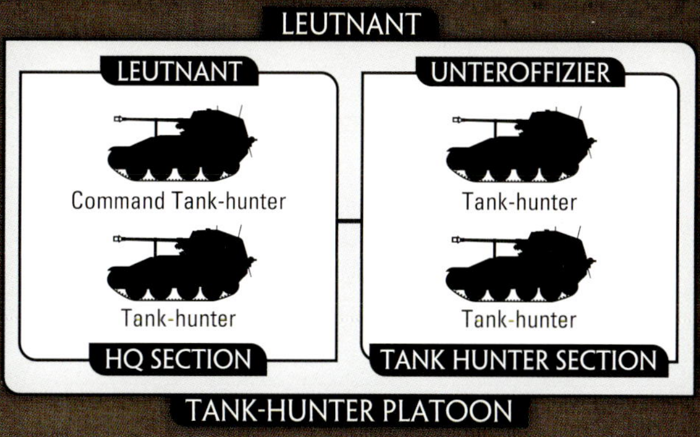

Marder III M

Armament: 7.5cm PaK40 gun, AA MG

Top Armour: 0 | **Front Armour:** 0 | **Side Armour:** 0 | **Movement:** Standard Tank

Weapon	Range	ROF	AT	FP	Notes
7.5cm PaK40 gun	*32"/80cm*	*2*	*12*	*3+*	*Hull mounted.*

Jagdpanzer IV

Armament: 7.5cm StuK40 gun, Hull MG, Protected ammo

Top Armour: 1 | **Front Armour:** 7 | **Side Armour:** 3 Schürzen | **Movement:** Standard Tank

Weapon	Range	ROF	AT	FP	Notes
7.5cm StuK40 gun	*32"/80cm*	*2*	*11*	*3+*	*Hull mounted.*

Hornisse

Armament: 8.8cm PaK43 gun, AA MG, Protected ammo

Top Armour: 0 | **Front Armour:** 1 | **Side Armour:** 1 | **Movement:** Standard Tank

Weapon	Range	ROF	AT	FP	Notes
8.8cm PaK43 gun	*40"/100cm*	*2*	*16*	*3+*	*Hull mounted.*

Jagdpanther

Armament: 8.8cm PaK43 gun, Hull MG

Top Armour: 1 | **Front Armour:** 10 | **Side Armour:** 5 | **Movement:** Standard Tank

Weapon	Range	ROF	AT	FP	Notes
8.8cm PaK43 gun	*40"/100cm*	*2*	*16*	*3+*	*Hull mounted.*

Assault Gun Platoon

Platoon

Platoon		
4 StuG G	380 points	435 points
3 StuG G	285 points	325 points
2 StuG G	190 points	215 points
4 StuH 42	380 points	-
3 StuH 42	285 points	-
2 StuH 42	190 points	-
4 Brummbär	280 points	-
3 Brummbär	210 points	-
2 Brummbär	140 points	-

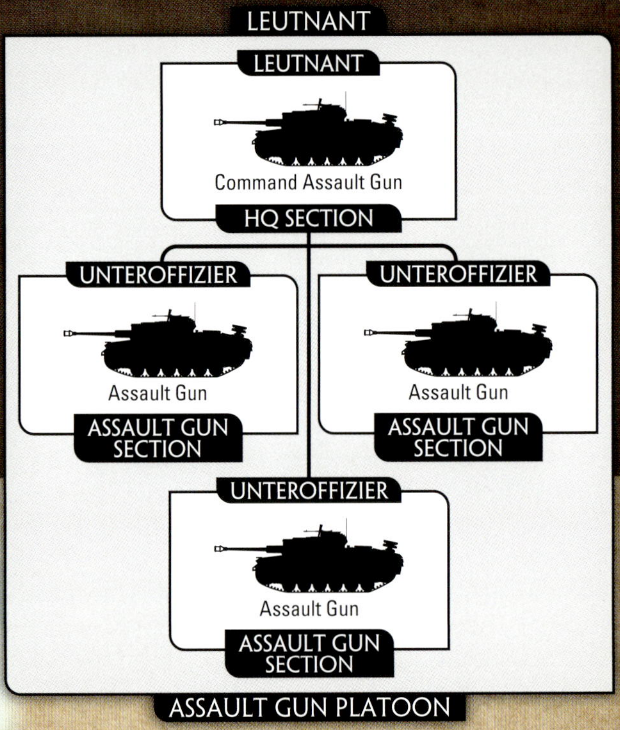

StuG G

Armament: 7.5cm StuK40 gun, Hull MG, Protected ammo

Top Armour: 1

Front Armour: 7

Movement: Standard Tank

Side Armour: 3 Schürzen

Weapon	*Range*	*ROF*	*AT*	*FP*	*Notes*
7.5cm StuK40 gun	*32"/80cm*	*2*	*11*	*3+*	*Hull mounted.*

Assault Guns

While the armoured troops were supported by tanks, the foot slogging Grenadiers were usually supported by their own armour, the assault guns. These weapons were designed to provide direct support to the infantry and were not fitted with turrets that tanks required for the quick direction changes of mobile warfare. Usually well armoured they supported the infantry in both attack and defence with mobile firepower that could be brought to bear where it was most needed.

StuH 42

Armament: 10.5cm StuH42 gun, Hull MG, Protected ammo

Top Armour: 1

Front Armour: 7

Movement: Standard Tank

Side Armour: 3 Schürzen

Weapon	*Range*	*ROF*	*AT*	*FP*	*Notes*
10.5cm StuH42	*32"/80cm*	*2*	*10*	*2+*	*Hull mounted, Breakthrough gun, Smoke.*

Brummbär

Top Armour: 1

Armament: 15cm StuH43 gun, Hull MG

Side Armour: 5 Schürzen

Movement: Overloaded, Slow tank

Front Armour: 9

Weapon	*Range*	*ROF*	*AT*	*FP*	*Notes*
15cm StuH43 gun	*16"/40cm*	*1*	*13*	*1+*	*Bunker buster, Hull mounted.*

PANZERSPÄH PATROL

PLATOON

Platoon	(Heer)	(SS)
2 Sd Kfz 231 (8-rad)	80 points	90 points
3 Sd Kfz 234/2 (Puma)	150 points	-
3 Panzer II L Luchs	145 points	-
1 Sd Kfz 223 (radio) & 2 Sd Kfz 222 (2cm)	110 points	120 points
1 Sd Kfz 250 (Recon) & 2 Sd Kfz 250/9 (2cm)	115 points	130 points

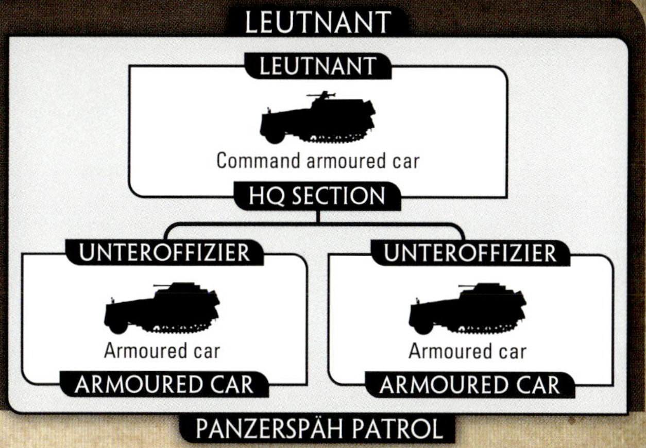

Panzerspäh Patrols are Reconnaissance Platoons (see pages 193 to 195 of the rulebook).

HEAVY ANTI-AIRCRAFT GUN PLATOON

PLATOON

HQ Section with:	(Heer)	(SS)
2 8.8cm FlaK36	160 points	185 points
1 8.8cm FlaK36	80 points	95 points

OPTIONS

- Model 8.8cm FlaK36 guns with eight or more crew and increase their ROF to 3 for +10 points per gun.
- Add Kfz 15 field car and Sd Kfz 7 half-tracks for +5 points for the platoon.

8.8CM FLAK36 GUN

Weapon	Range	ROF	AT	FP
8.8cm FlaK36 gun	*40"/100cm*	*2/3*	*13*	*3+*

ARNOLD HÜBNER, '88' ACE

Arnold Hübner first made a name for himself in the fighting in Libya in 1941. In his first ground combat he easily made the transition from shooting at aircraft to shooting at enemy tanks.

Hübner's unit, *3. Batterie I/Flak Regiment 33*, was in action in Libya in May 1941. From May 1941 until February 1942 he was in the thick of the fighting earning 1st and 2nd Class Iron Crosses and a Knight's Cross for his excellent gunnery.

In one example in December 1941 Hübner was in the thick of the action manning his gun against British Operation Crusader. During the fighting Hübner destroyed eight enemy tanks, to bring his personal total to 24 during 1941. His calmness under fire allowed him to carefully select his targets, making every shot count.

In February Flak Regiment 33 returned to Germany. On 7 March 1942 *Gefreiter* Arnold Hübner received his Knight's Cross in a ceremony at the regiment's barracks in Leipzig.

Hübner continued to serve, after a brief stint in hospital for a tropical disease he picked up in Africa, and worked his way through the NCO ranks. He served in Normandy and with anti-aircraft units in Germany. He ended the war in May 1945, just after a promotion to *Leutnant*, as a prisoner of war with the Americans.

Artillery Battery

Platoon

HQ Section with:

4 10.5cm leFH18	210 points	240 points
2 10.5cm leFH18	115 points	130 points
4 15cm sFH18	310 points	360 points
2 15cm sFH18	160 points	185 points

Options

- Add RSO tractors for +5 points for the battery.
- Replace Gun Section RSO tractors with Kfz 11 half-tracks, replace the HQ Section RSO tractor with a Kfz 15 field car and a Kfz 68 radio truck, and add Kübelwagen jeeps at no cost.
- Replace all Kübelwagen jeeps with Sd Kfz 250 half-tracks for +5 points per half-track.
- Replace any or all Observer Rifle teams and their Kübelwagen jeep with Observer Panzer II OP tanks for +10 points per tank.

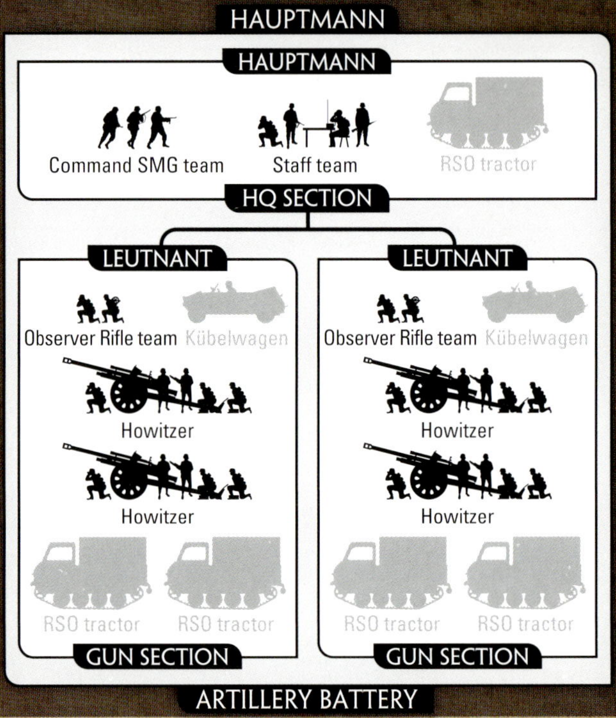

Armoured Artillery Battery

Platoon

HQ Section with:

6 Wespe	435 points	470 points
4 Wespe	315 points	340 points
3 Wespe	235 points	255 points
2 Wespe	170 points	180 points
6 Hummel	560 points	615 points
4 Hummel	405 points	440 points
3 Hummel	300 points	330 points
2 Hummel	210 points	230 points

Option

- Replace any or all Observer Rifle teams and their Sd Kfz 250 half-track with Observer Panzer III OP tanks for +5 points per tank.

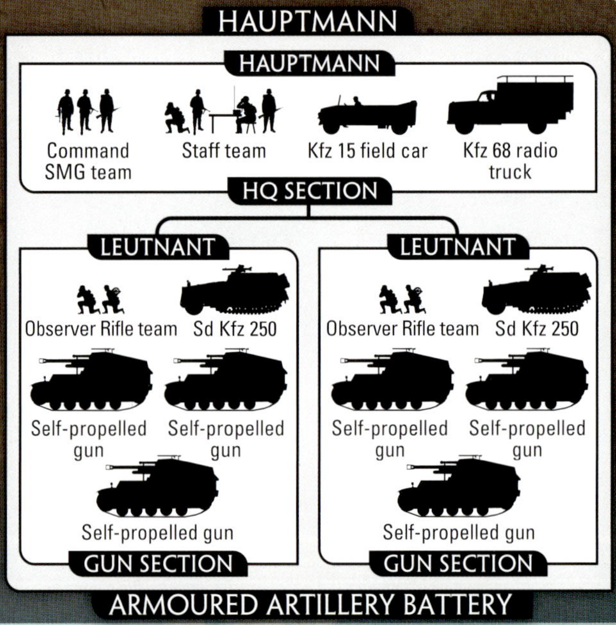

Wespe

Weapon	Range	ROF	AT	FP	Notes
10.5cm leFH18M howitzer	24"/60cm	1	10	2+	Hull mounted, Breakthrough gun, Smoke.
Firing bombardments	72"/180cm	-	4	4+	Smoke bombardment.

Hummel

Weapon	Range	ROF	AT	FP	Notes
15cm sFH18 howitzer	24"/60cm	1	13	1+	Bunker buster Hull mounted, Smoke.
Firing bombardments	80"/200cm	-	5	2+	Smoke bombardment.

German Arsenal

TANK TEAMS

Name *Weapon*	Mobility *Range*	Front *ROF*	Armour Side *Anti-tank*	Top *Firepower*	Equipment and Notes
TANKS					
Panzer IV H *7.5cm KwK40 gun*	Standard Tank *32"/80cm*	6 *2*	3 *11*	1 *3+*	Co-ax MG, Hull MG, Protected ammo, Schürzen.
Panther A *7.5cm KwK42 gun*	Standard Tank *32"/80cm*	10 *2*	5 *14*	1 *3+*	Co-ax MG, Hull MG, Wide tracks.
HEAVY TANKS					
Tiger I E *8.8cm KwK36 gun*	Slow Tank *40"/100cm*	9 *2*	8 *13*	2 *3+*	Co-ax MG, Hull MG, Protected ammo, Wide tracks. *Slow traverse.*
Königstiger (Henschel) *8.8cm KwK43 gun*	Slow Tank *40"/100cm*	15 *2*	8 *16*	2 *3+*	Co-ax MG, Hull MG, Overloaded. *Slow traverse.*
ASSAULT GUNS					
StuG G *7.5cm StuK40 gun*	Standard Tank *32"/80cm*	7 *2*	3 *11*	1 *3+*	Hull MG, Protected ammo, Schürzen. *Hull mounted.*
StuH42 *10.5cm StuH42 gun*	Standard Tank *32"/80cm*	7 *2*	3 *10*	1 *2+*	Hull MG, Protected ammo, Schürzen. *Hull mounted, Breakthrough gun, Smoke.*
Brummbär *15cm StuH43 gun*	Slow Tank *16"/40cm*	9 *1*	5 *13*	1 *1+*	Hull MG, Overloaded, Schürzen. *Bunker buster, Hull mounted.*
INFANTRY GUNS (SP)					
Sd Kfz 251/2 (8cm) half-track *8cm GW34 mortar* *Firing bombardments*	Half-tracked *24"/60cm* *40"/100cm*	1 *2* *-*	0 *2* *2*	0 *3+* *6*	AA MG. *Hull mounted, Portee, Smoke, Minimum range 8"/20cm.* *Smoke bombardment.*
Sd Kfz 251/9 (7.5cm) half-track *7.5cm KwK37 gun*	Half-tracked *24"/60cm*	1 *2*	0 *9*	0 *3+*	AA MG. *Hull mounted.*
Grille K (15cm sIG) *15cm sIG33 gun* *Firing bombardments*	Standard Tank *16"/40cm* *56"/140cm*	0 *1* *-*	0 *13* *4*	0 *1+* *2+*	AA MG. *Bunker buster, Hull mounted.*
TANK-HUNTERS					
Marder III M *7.5cm PaK40 gun*	Standard Tank *32"/80cm*	0 *2*	0 *12*	0 *3+*	AA MG. *Hull mounted.*
Jagdpanzer IV *7.5cm StuK40 gun*	Standard Tank *32"/80cm*	7 *2*	3 *11*	1 *3+*	Hull MG, Protected ammo, Schürzen. *Hull mounted.*
Hornisse *8.8cm PaK43 gun*	Standard Tank *40"/100cm*	1 *2*	1 *16*	0 *3+*	AA MG, Protected ammo. *Hull mounted.*
Jagdpanther *8.8cm PaK43 gun*	Standard Tank *40"/100cm*	10 *2*	5 *16*	1 *3+*	Hull MG. *Hull mounted.*

Name *Weapon*	Mobility *Range*	Front *ROF*	Armour Side *Anti-tank*	Top *Firepower*	Equipment and Notes

Reconnaissance

Name *Weapon*	Mobility *Range*	Front *ROF*	Side *Anti-tank*	Top *Firepower*	Equipment and Notes
Sd Kfz 222 (2cm)	Wheeled	1	0	0	Co-ax MG.
2cm KwK38 gun	*16"/40cm*	*3*	*5*	*5+*	*Self-defence anti-aircraft.*
Sd Kfz 223 (Radio)	Wheeled	1	0	0	AA MG.
Sd Kfz 231 (8-rad)	Jeep	2	0	0	Co-ax MG.
2cm KwK38 gun	*16"/40cm*	*3*	*5*	*5+*	
Sd Kfz 234/2 Puma	Jeep	3	0	0	Co-ax MG.
5cm KwK39 gun	*24"/60cm*	*2*	*9*	*4+*	
Sd Kfz 250 (Recon)	Half-tracked	1	0	0	Hull MG, AA MG.
Sd Kfz 250/9 (2cm)	Half-tracked	1	0	0	Co-ax MG.
2cm KwK38 gun	*16"/40cm*	*3*	*5*	*5+*	*Self-defence anti-aircraft.*
Panzer II L Luchs	Light Tank	3	1	1	Co-ax MG.
2cm KwK38 gun	*16"/40cm*	*3*	*5*	*5+*	

Artillery (SP)

Name *Weapon*	Mobility *Range*	Front *ROF*	Side *Anti-tank*	Top *Firepower*	Equipment and Notes
Wespe	Standard Tank	1	1	0	AA MG, Protected ammo.
10.5cm leFH18M howitzer	*24"/60cm*	*1*	*10*	*2+*	*Breakthrough gun, Hull mounted, Smoke.*
Firing bombardments	*72"/180cm*	-	*4*	*4+*	*Smoke bombardment.*
Hummel	Standard Tank	1	1	0	AA MG, Protected ammo.
15cm sFH18 howitzer	*24"/60cm*	*1*	*13*	*1+*	*Bunker buster, Hull mounted, Smoke.*
Firing bombardments	*80"/200cm*	-	*5*	*2+*	*Smoke bombardment.*
Panzer II OP	Standard Tank	3	1	1	Co-ax MG, Protected ammo.
2cm KwK38 gun	*16"/40cm*	*3*	*5*	*5+*	
Panzer III OP	Standard Tank	5	3	1	Hull MG.

Anti-aircraft (SP)

Name *Weapon*	Mobility *Range*	Front *ROF*	Side *Anti-tank*	Top *Firepower*	Equipment and Notes
Sd Kfz 10/5 (2cm)	Half-tracked	-	-	-	Gun shield.
2cm FlaK38 gun	*16"/40cm*	*4*	*5*	*5+*	*Anti-aircraft.*
Armoured Sd Kfz 10/5 (2cm)	Half-tracked	0	0	0	
2cm FlaK38 gun	*16"/40cm*	*4*	*5*	*5+*	*Anti-aircraft.*
Sd Kfz 7/1 (Quad 2cm)	Half-tracked	-	-	-	Gun shield.
2cm FlaK38 (V) gun	*16"/40cm*	*6*	*5*	*5+*	*Anti-aircraft.*
Armoured Sd Kfz 7/1 (Quad 2cm)	Half-tracked	0	0	0	
2cm FlaK38 (V) gun	*16"/40cm*	*6*	*5*	*5+*	*Anti-aircraft.*

GUN TEAMS

Weapon	Mobility	Range	ROF	Anti-tank	Firepower	Notes
MG42 HMG	Man-packed	24"/60cm	6	2	6	ROF 3 when pinned down or moving.
8cm GW34 mortar	Man-packed	24"/60cm	2	2	3+	Smoke, Minimum range 8"/20cm.
Firing bombardments		40"/100cm	-	2	6	Smoke bombardment.
12cm sGW43 mortar	Light	56"/140cm	-	3	3+	
7.5cm leIG18 gun	Light	16"/40cm	2	9	3+	Gun shield, Smoke.
Firing bombardments		48"/120cm	-	3	6	
15cm sIG33 gun	Heavy	16"/40cm	1	13	1+	Bunker buster, Gun shield.
Firing bombardments		56"/140cm	-	4	2+	
7.5cm PaK40 gun	Medium	32"/80cm	2	12	3+	Gun shield.
8.8cm FlaK36 gun	Immobile	40"/100cm	2	13	3+	Gun shield, Heavy anti-aircraft, Turntable.
10.5cm leFH18 howitzer	Immobile	24"/60cm	1	10	2+	Gun shield, Breakthrough gun, Smoke.
Firing bombardments		72"/180cm	-	4	4+	Smoke bombardment.
15cm sFH18 howitzer	Immobile	24"/60cm	1	13	1+	Bunker buster, Smoke.
Firing bombardments		80"/200cm	-	5	2+	Smoke bombardment.

TRANSPORT TEAMS

Vehicle *Weapon*	Mobility *Range*	Armour Front *ROF*	Armour Side *Anti-tank*	Armour Top *Firepower*	Equipment and Notes
Trucks					
BMW motorcycle & sidecar or Kübelwagen	Jeep	-	-	-	
Horch Kfz 15 field car	Jeep	-	-	-	
Steyr Kfz 70 truck,	Wheeled	-	-	-	
Opel Blitz 3-ton truck	Wheeled	-	-	-	
Opel Maultier	Half-tracked	-	-	-	
Opel Kfz 68 radio truck	Wheeled	-	-	-	
Tractors					
Sd Kfz 11, or Sd Kfz 7 half-track	Half-tracked	-	-	-	
RSO tractor	Slow Tank	-	-	-	
Armoured Personnel Carriers					
Sd Kfz 250 half-track	Half-tracked	1	0	0	Hull MG, Passenger-fired AA MG.
Sd Kfz 251/1 half-track	Half-tracked	1	0	0	Hull MG, Passenger-fired AA MG.
Sd Kfz 251/1 (HMG) half-track	Half-tracked	1	0	0	Hull MG, HMG Carrier, Passenger-fired AA MG.
Sd Kfz 251/7 (Pioneer) half-track	Half-tracked	1	0	0	Hull MG, Passenger-fired AA MG, Assault bridge.
Sd Kfz 251/10 (3.7cm) half-track	Half-tracked	1	0	0	Passenger-fired AA MG.
3.7cm PaK36 gun	*16"/40cm*	*2*	*6*	*4+*	*Hull mounted.*

INFANTRY TEAMS

Team	Range	ROF	Anti-tank	Firepower	Notes
Rifle team	16"/40cm	1	2	6	
Rifle/MG team	16"/40cm	2	2	6	
MG team	16"/40cm	3	2	6	ROF 2 when pinned down.
SMG team	4"/10cm	3	1	6	Full ROF when moving.
Panzerschreck team	8"/20cm	2	11	5+	Tank Assault 5.
Flame-thrower team	4"/10cm	2	-	6	Flame-thrower.
Observer Rifle team	16"/40cm	1	2	6	Observer.
Staff team		cannot shoot			Moves as a Heavy Gun team
Additional Training and Equipment					
Panzerfaust	4"/10cm	1	12	5+	Tank Assault 6, Cannot shoot in the Shooting Step if moved in the Movement Step.

Pioneer teams are rated as Tank Assault 4. Panzerknacker teams are rated as Tank Assault 5.

AIRCRAFT

Aircraft	Weapon	To Hit	Anti-tank	Firepower	Notes
Ju 87D Stuka	Bombs	4+	5	1+	
Ju 87G Stuka	Cannon	3+	11	4+	
Hs 129B	Cannon	2+	9	4+	Flying Tank

The German *Luftwaffe*, or Air Force, supported the troops of the *Heer* and *SS* with sorties of ground attack aircraft. The Germans used Ju 87D Stuka dive-bombers, and Ju 87G and Hs 129B tank-busters in this role.

Ju 87D Stuka dive bomber carries bombs which are ideal for saturating an area of attack. They are not as accurate as cannon-armed aircraft, but they destroy any soft targets they hit. They are also effective against armoured targets as their bombs rain down on vulnerable top armour.

The cannon-armed Ju 87G Stuka and Hs 129B are designed to knock out tanks. They come in low where their cannon fire at the vehicles side armour. They are more accurate than bombs, and their good Anti-tank rating means they slice through the side armour of most tanks. However, their lower Firepower rating means they don't always destroy every tank.

Hs 129B has additional armour and can fly through the heaviest of anti-aircraft fire and still deliver its terrible volley on the enemy tanks.

British Forces, 1944

'We shall defend our island, whatever the cost may be, we shall fight on the beaches, we shall fight on the landing grounds, we shall fight in the fields and in the streets, we shall fight in the hills, we shall never surrender.'

—Prime Minister Winston S Churchill

From across the world you sons of England have come to fight for King and Country, your bravery will echo across the ages as did that of your ancestors at Agincourt and Waterloo. The weapons may be different but, by jove, the determination and bravery of this generation will prove the equal of any other in the history of the Empire. Rule Britannia!

Now listen up chaps, we all know that no upstart Hun and his goose-stepping cronies can challenge the might of the British Empire. Ahh…what a glorious empire it is—stretching from the shores of the mother country, across the grasslands of South Africa and the jewel that is India to the south sea colonies of Australia and New Zealand and on to the vast wilderness of Canada. The sun never sets on the British Empire.

You lucky young chaps are about to become a part of the British Army, so let me tell you a thing or two about the proud regiments you are about to join. The Regimental system is an ancient tradition, dating back to the Civil War. Each Regiment draws on the manpower of a county to maintain its strength —you at the back, pay attention! The regiments breed a fierce loyalty amongst their men. Normally, one battalion is kept at home forming while the other is deployed overseas. Of course in desperate times like these, every man is needed at the front. I know you chaps are just itching to get at the Nazi swine. Don't worry. You'll soon get your chance!

Now tradition plays a big part, but the British Army of today is at the leading edge of modern mechanised warfare. We've finally got rid of the old fuddy-duddies who thought we'd be refighting the First War in trenches. Things have moved on. We've got the equipment and the tactics to give Jerry another damn good thrashing!

Unlike many armies, who tend to go on about the exploits of their cavalry and artillery, the British Army has always honoured the bravery and daring of its proud infantry regiments. Truly, they do not fail or falter; they do not weaken or tire—the British infantry is indomitable! The backbone of the infantry are the Non-Commissioned Officers (NCOs)—long-serving professional soldiers. It is said that the British NCO believes in only three things – discipline, discipline, and discipline, as I'm sure you'll all soon discover.

The infantry's job is made easier by the first-class support available to them, not the least of which is from the Royal Artillery. The artillery chappies are very clever indeed and have come up with many innovative ways to blast the stuffing out of the Hun. The German soldier is well aware that if he wants to get at the British soldier he must first survive a frightful snotting from the British guns. Jerry never gets one without the other.

Of course old Jerry likes to make quite a fuss over his Panzers! But the tank is a British invention and we've got just the sort

to send those Panzers packing. Our tanks are organised into squadrons—originally they were horse-mounted cavalry squadrons, you see. In fact, the armoured squadrons still have a slight tendency to think like cavalry, and had a deplorable penchant for launching a frontal assault on well-defended enemy positions at the drop of a hat. 'Into the Valley of Death rode the six hundred...' and all that! 100 years ago it may have worked, but not today. So the tank chaps have had to learn to add a dash of cunning to go with their evident bravery. The scoreboard is looking a lot more even these days and the Hun is not too happy about the pasting he's starting to get. Serves the little blighter right, I say!

No doubt you chaps have heard of the bold exploits of our Commandos—ha-ha, Adolph certainly has! It was these fellows who first took the war back to Germany on the continent with their daring raids. And now they continue to be a thorn in the side of the Huns.

Let's not forget the invaluable service rendered by troops from the nations of the British Empire too—Canadian, Indian, Australian, New Zealand and South African fellows for the most part. We've also got troops from countries overrun by the Nazis who are thirsting for revenge, like the Poles, French and Czechs. These chaps may do things a little differently from our boys but they are every bit as brave and equally well trained.

The British Army has been fighting and winning wars for hundreds of years. In that time we've taken the best that our foes have thrown at us and the army has always come out on top. What more proof is needed of the superior character and training of the British soldier? None I say! And Jerry is beginning to rediscover the lesson we gave him in the First World War—that the British Army will not give an inch to some ghastly upstart Hun who thinks he can carve himself an empire in Europe.

ARMOURED SQUADRON

(ARMOURED COMPANY)

RELUCTANT	CONSCRIPT
CONFIDENT	**TRAINED**
FEARLESS	VETERAN

TANK COMPANY

HEADQUARTERS

HEADQUARTERS

Company Command Sherman V — 2iC Command Sherman V — Sherman V — Sherman V

Armoured Squadron HQ

HEADQUARTERS

Company HQ with:

4 Sherman V	265 points
3 Sherman V	200 points
2 Sherman V	135 points

OPTION

- Arm any or all Sherman tanks with a .50 cal AA MG for +5 points per tank.

COMBAT PLATOONS

- ARMOUR — Armoured Platoon (59)
- ARMOUR — Armoured Platoon (59)
- ARMOUR — Armoured Platoon (59)
- ARMOUR — Armoured Platoon (59)

WEAPONS PLATOONS

- RECONNAISSANCE — Recce Patrol (59)

BRIGADE SUPPORT PLATOONS

- RECONNAISSANCE — Scout Platoon (61)
- INFANTRY — Motor Platoon (61); Rifle Platoon (65)
- RECONNAISSANCE — Armoured Car Platoon (71)

DIVISIONAL SUPPORT PLATOONS

- ANTI-TANK — Anti-tank Platoon (SP), Royal Artillery (69)
- ARTILLERY — Field Battery (SP), Royal Artillery (71)
- INFANTRY — Parachute Rifle Platoon (17)
- ARTILLERY — Field Battery, Royal Artillery (70); Field Battery (SP), Royal Artillery (71); Medium Battery, Royal Artillery (72)
- AIRCRAFT — Air Support (73)

ALLIED PLATOONS

US Platoons in your force are Allies and follow the Allies rules on page 70 of the rulebook.

SHERMAN V

Armament: M3 75mm gun, Co-ax MG, Hull MG

Top Armour: 1

Front Armour: 6

Side Armour: 4

Movement: Standard Tank, Tow hook

Weapon	Range	ROF	AT	FP	Notes
M3 75mm gun	32"/80cm	2	10	3+	Semi-indirect fire, Smoke.

COMBAT PLATOONS

ARMOURED PLATOON

PLATOON

3 Sherman V & 1 Firefly VC	280 points
2 Sherman V & 1 Firefly VC	215 points

OPTION

- Arm any or all Sherman or Firefly tanks with a .50 cal AA MG for +5 points per tank.

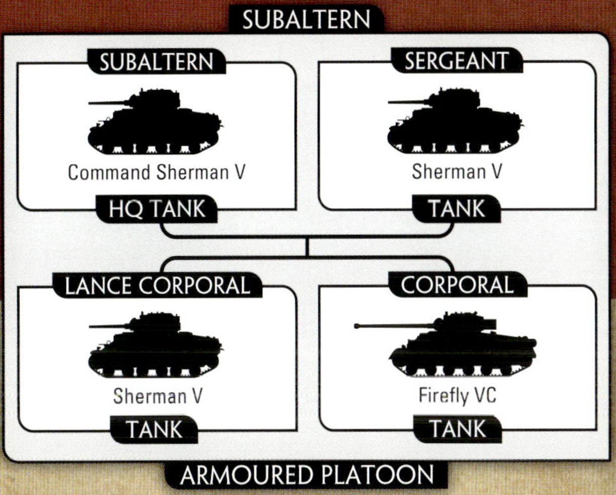

At the core of your Armoured Squadron are the sturdy American Sherman tanks. The versatile 75mm-armed model is supplemented by the Firefly, a British-modified Sherman armed with the powerful 17 pdr gun to counter the Germans' new heavy Tiger and the Panther tanks. This combination of firepower and reliability is more than enough to deal with anything the enemy have.

SEMI-INDIRECT FIRE

British heavy tanks often open fire at very long ranges, where their prolific use of ammunition can compensate for the difficulty of hitting the target. It means that their ammo racks empty fast, but there's plenty more available to resupply. In Flames Of War British tanks with guns capable of Semi-indirect Fire can re-roll failed rolls to hit, as long as they didn't move in the Movement Step. This is only when shooting their main guns at platoons over 16"/40cm away.

WEAPONS PLATOONS

RECCE PATROL

PLATOON

4 Stuart V	160 points
3 Stuart V	120 points

OPTIONS

- Arm any or all Stuart tanks with an AA MG for +5 points per tank.
- Modify any or all Stuart tanks into Stuart Jalopies for -5 points per tank.

Recce Patrols are Reconnaissance Platoons (see pages 193 to 195 of the rulebook).

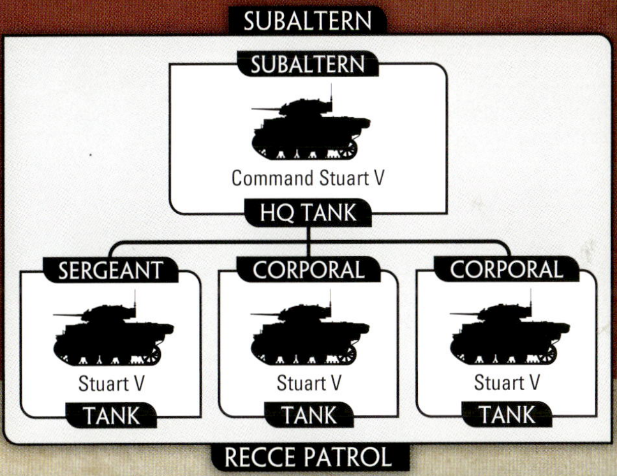

FIREFLY VC

Weapon	Range	ROF	AT	FP	Notes
OQF 17 pdr gun	32"/80cm	2	13	3+	No HE, Semi-indirect fire.

STUART V

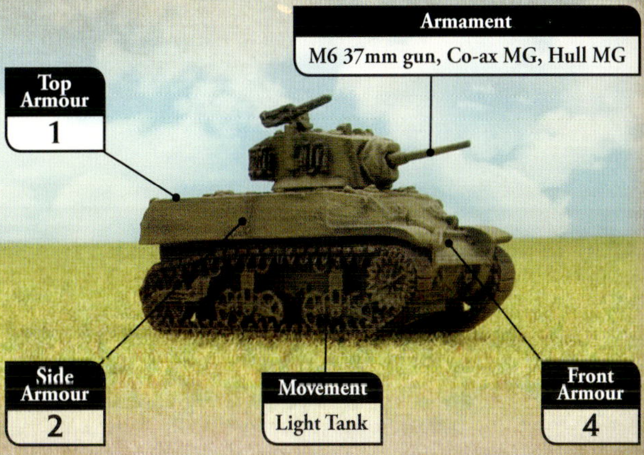

Weapon	Range	ROF	AT	FP	Notes
M6 37mm gun	24"/60cm	2	7	4+	

Motor Company

RELUCTANT | CONSCRIPT
CONFIDENT | TRAINED
FEARLESS | VETERAN

Infantry Company

Headquarters

HEADQUARTERS

Company Command Rifle team — White scout car

2iC Command Rifle team — White scout car

CORPORAL

3" mortar — White scout car — 3" mortar — White scout car

MORTAR SECTION

Motor Company HQ

Headquarters

Company HQ	25 points

Option

- Add a Mortar Section for +40 points.

The riflemen of the motor companies support the armoured squadrons admirably. Riding into battle aboard their American-made M5 half-tracks, the resolute riflemen will consolidate the gains made by the tanks or even, if terrain is restricting the movement of the tanks, lead the way into the enemy positions. They are ably supported by the tanks and the guns of their division.

Combat Platoons

INFANTRY — Motor Platoon 61

INFANTRY — Motor Platoon 61

INFANTRY — Motor Platoon 61

RECONNAISSANCE — Scout Platoon 61

Weapons Platoons

MACHINE-GUNS — Motor Machine-gun Platoon 62

ANTI-TANK — Motor Anti-tank Platoon 62

ANTI-TANK — Motor Anti-tank Platoon 62

Allied Platoons

US Platoons in your force are Allies and follow the Allies rules on page 70 of the rulebook.

Divisional Support Platoons

ARMOUR — Armoured Platoon 59; Anti-tank Platoon (SP), Royal Artillery 69

ARMOUR — Armoured Platoon 59; Anti-tank Platoon (SP), Royal Artillery 69

RECONNAISSANCE — Armoured Car Platoon 71

INFANTRY — Parachute Rifle Platoon 17

ARTILLERY — Field Battery (SP), Royal Artillery 71

ARTILLERY — Field Battery, Royal Artillery 70; Field Battery (SP), Royal Artillery 71; Medium Battery, Royal Artillery 72

AIRCRAFT — Air Support 73

COMBAT PLATOONS

MOTOR PLATOON

PLATOON

HQ Section with:

3 Motor Squads	110 points
2 Motor Squads	90 points

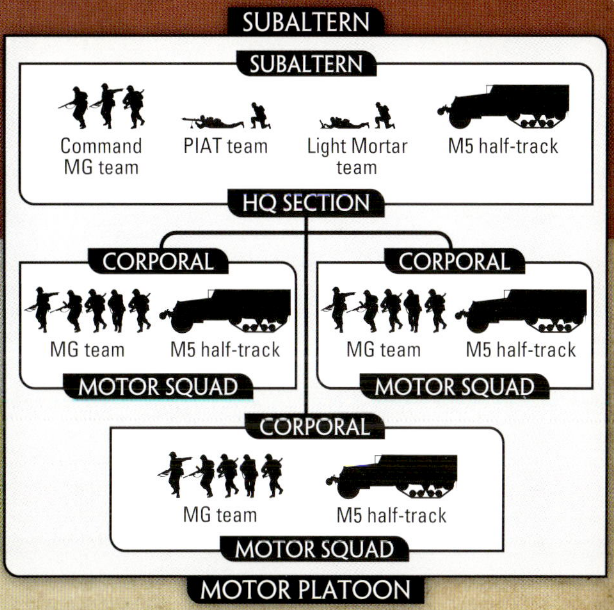

SCOUT PLATOON

PLATOON

3 Scout Patrols with:

9 Universal Carriers	200 points

2 Scout Patrols with:

6 Universal Carriers	135 points

1 Scout Patrol with:

3 Universal Carriers	70 points

OPTIONS

- Arm any or all Universal Carriers with an extra hull-mounted MG for +5 points per carrier or .50 cal MG for +10 points per carrier.
- Replace up to one extra hull-mounted MG with a PIAT anti-tank projector per Scout Patrol at no cost.

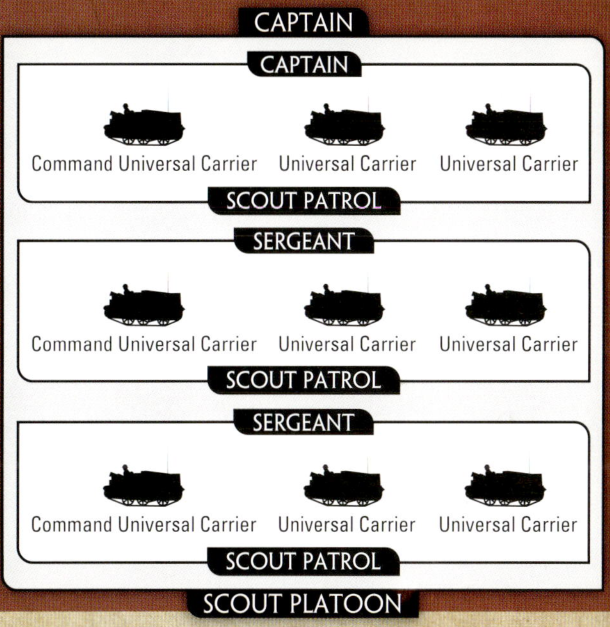

Scout Platoons are Reconnaissance Platoons (see pages 193 to 195 of the rulebook).

Scout Patrols of a Scout Platoon operate as separate platoons, each with their own command team.

WEAPONS PLATOONS

Motor Machine-gun Platoon

Platoon

HQ Section with:

4 Vickers (Motor)	100 points
2 Vickers (Motor)	55 points

Options

- Add PIAT team for +15 points.
- Add Troop Carrier and MMG Carriers to the platoon for +15 points per Machine-gun Section

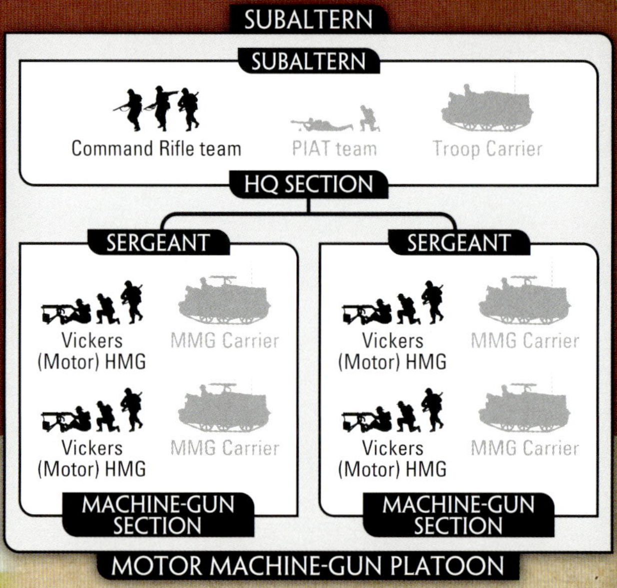

Vickers (motor) HMG

Notes: ROF 3 when pinned down or moving.

Movement: Man-packed

Weapon	Range	ROF	AT	FP
Vickers (Motor) HMG	*24"/60cm*	*6*	*2*	*6*

Motor Anti-tank Platoon

Platoon

HQ Section with:

4 OQF 6 pdr	100 points
2 OQF 6 pdr	50 points

Option

- Add Troop and Loyd Carriers for +5 points for the platoon.

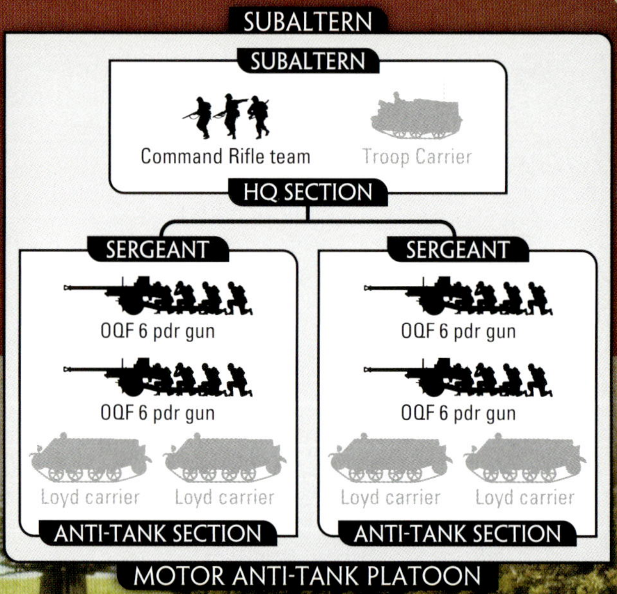

PLATOON FIREPOWER COMPARISONS

The firepower of an infantry platoon is mainly in its light machine-guns. These provide the bulk of the firepower, but require several soldiers to keep feeding them ammunition. The riflemen protect the machine-guns by covering areas that the machine-gun aren't, as well as carrying extra ammunition. NCO's and officers carry short-ranged submachine-guns or pistols to increase the platoon's firepower in close-combat, while allowing them to concentrate on commanding for the rest of the battle. Some platoons also had a short-ranged anti-tank weapon. The Germans used the disposable, one-shot *Panzerfaust* (armoured fist), while the British use the PIAT (Projector, Infantry, Anti-Tank).

GERMAN GRENADIER PLATOON FIREPOWER

The bulk of the German army consisted of the Grenadiers. A Grenadier Platoon has an excellent firepower base due to the excellent MG42 machine-gun with it's potential 1200 rounds per minute (RPM). This is not always achieved, but due to the MG42 machine-gun's belt-fed ammunition, of all the nations, this weapon get's the best out of its RPM. This firepower is backed up by the riflemen and submachine-gunners of the platoon.

9 x MP40 submachine-guns, 3 x MG42 machine-guns (three crew each), 12 x Kar98K rifles

BRITISH RIFLE PLATOON FIREPOWER

A British rifle platoon doesn't have the same immediate fire-power as a German platoon, but it carries the same amount of ammunition. This allows the British platoon to deliver its firepower at a more measured pace through out the battle.

The British platoon is versatile, having a light mortar for knocking out machine-gun nests and firing smoke, and a PIAT (Projector, Infantry, Anti-tank) for taking on tanks and bunkers.

4 x Sten submachine-guns, 3 x Bren machine-guns (two crew each), 22 x No. 4 rifles, 1 x PIAT (two crew), 1 x 2" mortar (two crew), 1 x Webley pistol

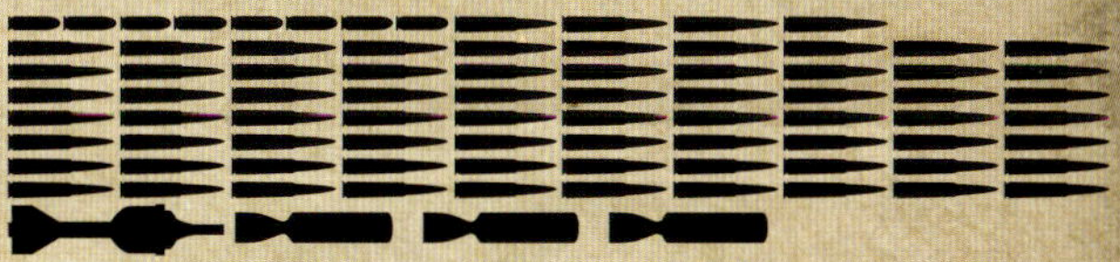

US RIFLE PLATOON FIREPOWER

US Rifle Platoons are bigger than those of the other nations and their firepower is further enhanced by the M1 Garand semi-automatic rifle. The semi-automatic weapon doesn't require the working of a bolt action to load another bullet ready for firing, the semi-automatic action does this for the GI. Backing up this enhanced firepower is the BAR. This older weapon is still capable of a good rate of fire, but requires frequent changes of its 20-round box magazine.

1 x M1 Carbine, 3 x Browning Automatic Rifle (two crew each), 32 x M1 Garand rifles, 1 x Bazooka (two crew)

SOVIET STRELKOVY COMPANY FIREPOWER

The Red Army is massive and though the individual firepower of each soldier may not add up to that of other nations, they have numbers on their side. Most of the time a Grenadier Platoon will be facing a Strelkovy Company with two or three platoons. Soviet firepower comes from DP machine-guns, rifles and submachine-guns, and sometimes Maksim heavy machine-guns. Some companies field one platoon completely armed with submachine-guns, massively increasing their short range firepower.

HQ: 1 x Tokarev TT33 Pistol, 1 x PPSh-41 submachine-gun, 1 x M1891/30 Rifle, 1x Maksim HMG.

3 Platoons with: 3 x PPSh-41 submachine-gun, 3 x DP machine-guns (two crew each), 25 x M1891/30 Rifle

Rifle Company

RELUCTANT | CONSCRIPT
CONFIDENT | TRAINED
FEARLESS | VETERAN

INFANTRY COMPANY

HEADQUARTERS

HEADQUARTERS

- Company Command Rifle team
- 2iC Command Rifle team
- Troop Carrier

Rifle Company HQ

Headquarters

Company HQ	25 points

Options

- Add Troop Carrier for +5 points.
- Add up to three Sniper teams for +50 points per team.

COMBAT PLATOONS

- INFANTRY — Rifle Platoon 65
- INFANTRY — Rifle Platoon 65
- INFANTRY — Rifle Platoon 65

WEAPONS PLATOONS

- ARTILLERY — Mortar Platoon 66
- ANTI-TANK — Anti-tank Platoon 66
- RECONNAISSANCE — Carrier Platoon 67

BRIGADE SUPPORT PLATOONS

- MACHINE-GUNS — Machine-gun Platoon 68
- MACHINE-GUNS — Machine-gun Platoon 68; Heavy Mortar Platoon 68

DIVISIONAL SUPPORT PLATOONS

- ARMOUR — Armoured Platoon 59; Tank Platoon 73
- ARMOUR — Armoured Platoon 59; Tank Platoon 73
- ANTI-TANK — Anti-tank Platoon (SP), Royal Artillery 69; Anti-tank Platoon, Royal Artillery 69; Heavy Anti-tank Platoon, Royal Artillery 69
- INFANTRY — Rifle Platoon 65; Parachute Rifle Platoon 17
- ARTILLERY — Field Battery, Royal Artillery 70
- ARTILLERY — Field Battery, Royal Artillery 70; Medium Battery, Royal Artillery 72
- AIRCRAFT — Air Support 73

ALLIED PLATOONS

US Platoons in your force are Allies and follow the Allies rules on page 70 of the rulebook.

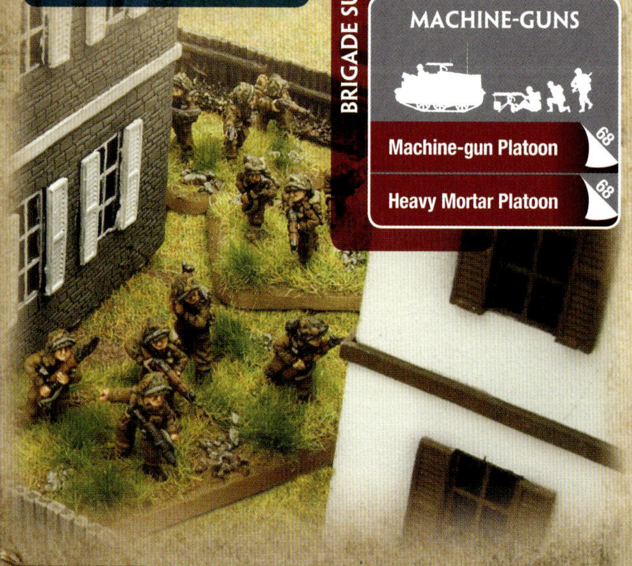

British Bulldog

Some 200 years ago, a French general remarked that the British troops his infantry attacked appeared to have taken root and be stuck to the ground. They refused to run away when other troops would have. Nothing has changed and British soldiers still have a reputation for tenacity and stubbornly refusing to give up ground that they have taken.

In Flames Of War when British platoons take a Motivation Test to Counterattack in assaults, you may re-roll the die and apply the re-rolled result to all British platoons that failed on the original roll. See page 246 of the *Flames Of War* rulebook.

Combat Platoons

Rifle Platoon

Platoon

HQ Section with:

3 Rifle Squads	140 points
2 Rifle Squads	110 points

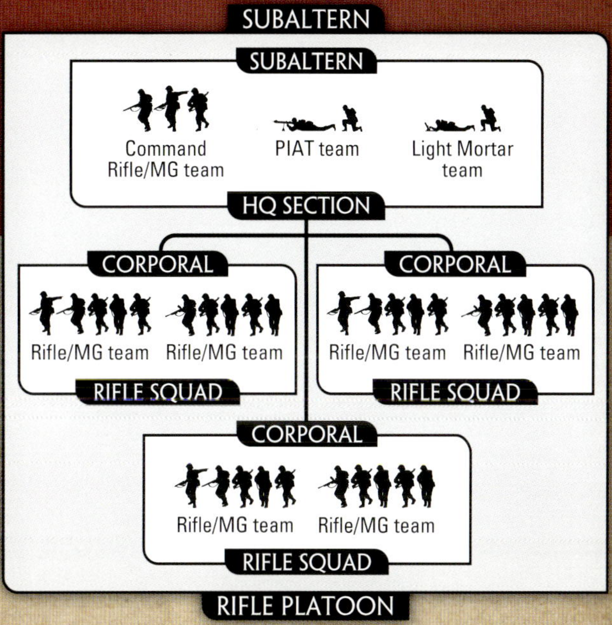

Solid and enduring in defence and implacable in the attack, the stout riflemen of the rifle company are the foundation for all other arms of the British Army. Well supported by artillery or tanks, it is the infantrymen that will storm that enemy positions at the point of a bayonet.

The riflemen have at their disposal a number of weapons in addition to their rifles and light machine-guns. They can keep enemy tanks at bay with the PIAT anti-tank projector. They also have a little 2-inch mortar providing covering smoke or high-explosive bombs against enemy entrenchments.

British Weapon Firepower

Weapon	Volume of fire and Range (0m – 500m)	Weight	Rate of Fire	Magazine	Range
Sten submachine-gun		6.6lb/3kg	550 rpm	Box (32)	50m
Bren machine-gun		22.3lb/10kg	500 rpm	Box (30)	500m
No. 4, Mk. 1 Rifle		9.1lb/4.1kg	60 rpm	Clip (10)	500m
PIAT		32lb/14.5kg	4 rpm	3lb/1.4kg per round	100m
2" mortar		19lb/8.6kg	8 rpm	2.3lb/1kg per round	500m
Webley revolver		1.8lb/0.8kg	20 rpm	Cylinder (6)	50m

WEAPONS PLATOONS

MORTAR PLATOON

PLATOON

HQ Section with:

6 ML 3" Mk II	135 points
4 ML 3" Mk II	90 points
2 ML 3" Mk II	45 points

OPTIONS

- Add PIAT teams for +15 points per team.
- Add Troop and Mortar Carriers for +5 points for the platoon.

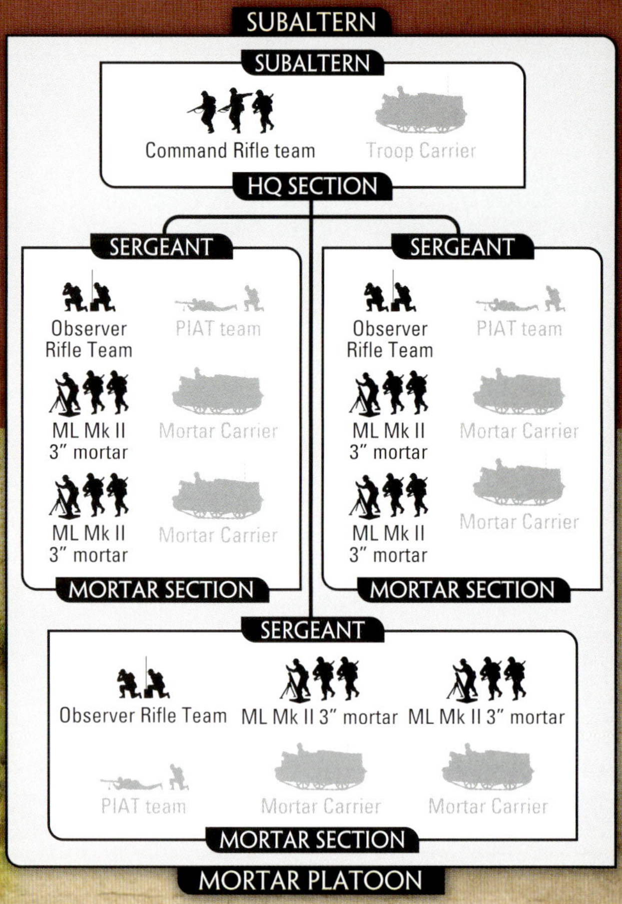

ANTI-TANK PLATOON

PLATOON

HQ Section with:

6 OQF 6 pdr	145 points
4 OQF 6 pdr	100 points
2 OQF 6 pdr	50 points

OPTION

- Add Troop and Loyd Carriers for +5 points for the platoon.

OQF 6 PDR GUN

Weapon	Range	ROF	AT	FP
OQF 6 pdr gun	24"/60cm	3	10	4+

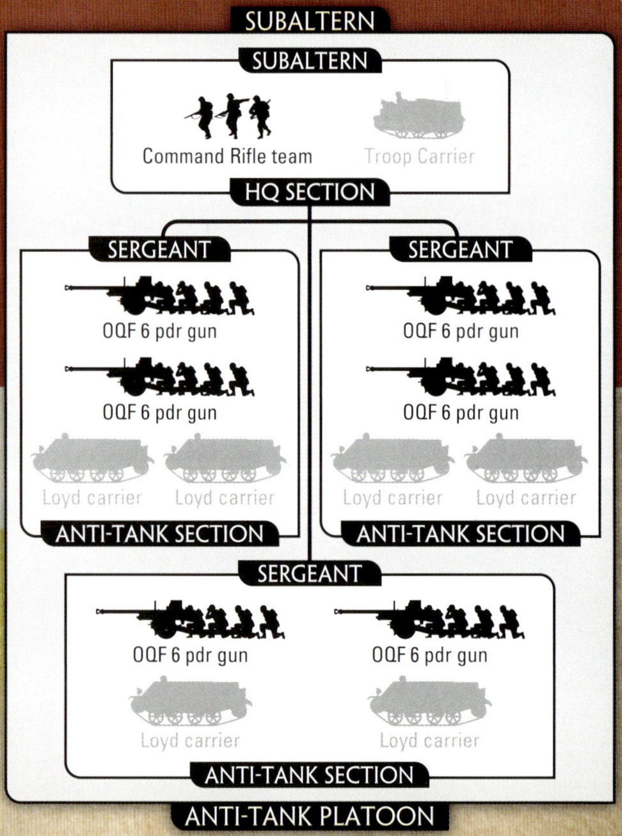

CARRIER PLATOON

PLATOON

4 Carrier Patrols with:

12 Universal Carriers	265 points

3 Carrier Patrols with:

9 Universal Carriers	200 points

2 Carrier Patrols with:

6 Universal Carriers	135 points

1 Carrier Patrol with:

3 Universal Carriers	70 points

OPTIONS

- Arm any or all Universal Carriers with an extra hull-mounted MG for +5 points per carrier or .50 cal MG for +10 points per carrier.
- Replace up to one extra hull-mounted MG with a PIAT anti-tank projector per Carrier Patrol at no cost.
- Replace all the Universal Carriers in up to two Carrier Patrols with Wasp Carriers for +25 points per Patrol.

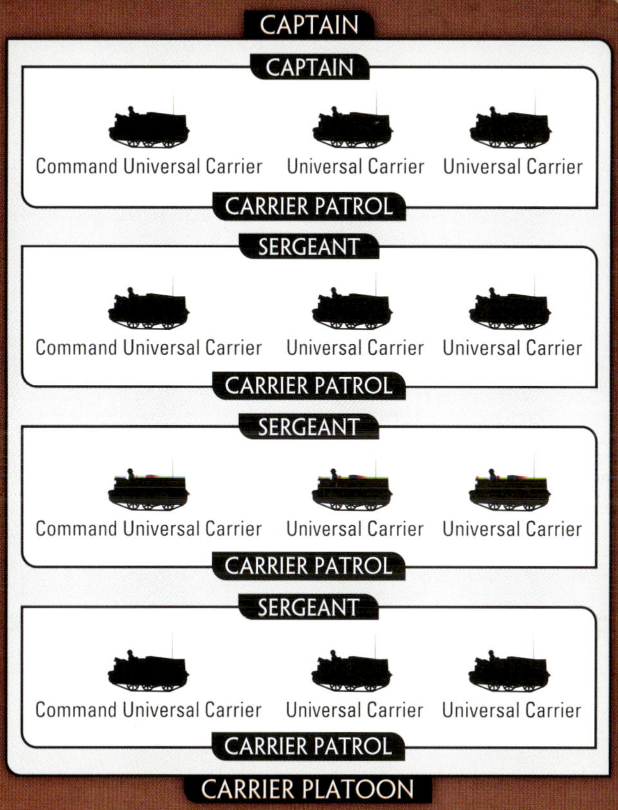

Carrier Patrols of a Carrier Platoon operate as separate platoons, each with their own command team.

Carrier Patrols equipped with Universal Carriers are Reconnaissance Platoons.

UNIVERSAL CARRIER

Weapon	Range	ROF	AT	FP	Notes
PIAT anti-tank projector	8"/20cm	1	10	5+	Hull-mounted.
.50 cal MG	16"/40cm	3	4	5+	Hull-mounted.

WASP CARRIER

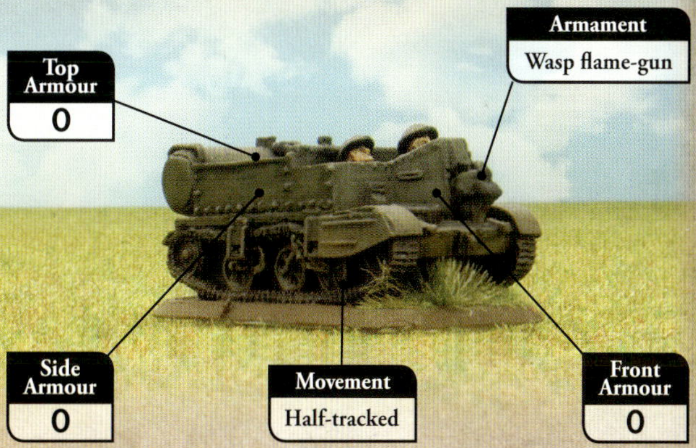

Weapon	Range	ROF	AT	FP	Notes
Wasp flame-gun	4"/10cm	3	-	6	Hull mounted, Flame-thrower.

BRIGADE SUPPORT PLATOONS

Machine-gun Platoon

Platoon

HQ Section with:

4 Vickers	110 points
2 Vickers	55 points

Options

- Add PIAT team for +15 points.
- Add Troop Carrier and MMG Carriers to the platoon for +15 points per Machine-gun Section

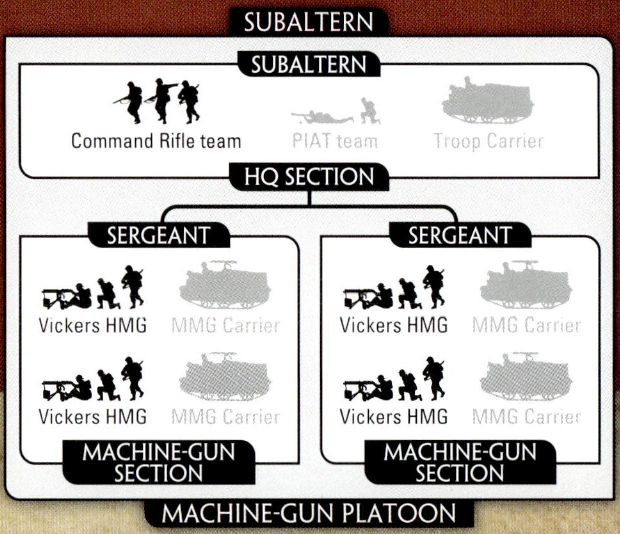

Heavy Mortar Platoon

Platoon

HQ Section with:

4 ML 4.2"	120 points
2 ML 4.2"	60 points

Options

- Add PIAT team for +15 points.
- Add Troop Carriers and Loyd Carriers for +5 points for the platoon.

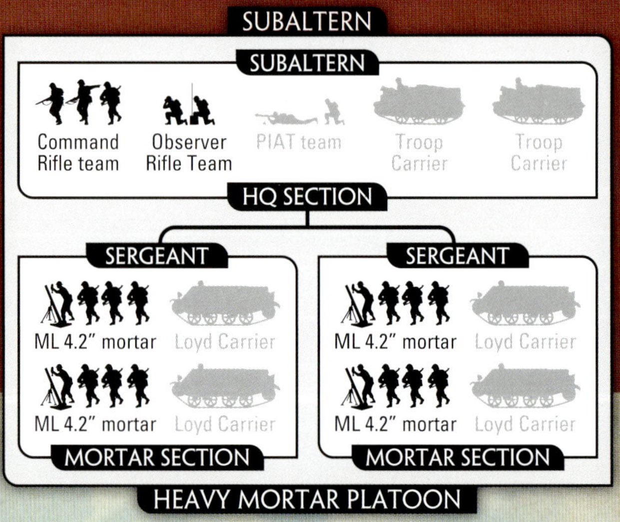

ML 3" Mk II mortar

Weapon	Range	ROF	AT	FP
ML 3" Mk II mortar	24"/60cm	2	2	3+
Firing bombardments	40"/100cm	-	2	6

ML 4.2" mortar

Weapon	Range	ROF	AT	FP
ML 4.2" mortar	48"/120cm	-	3	4+

DIVISIONAL SUPPORT

RELUCTANT	CONSCRIPT
CONFIDENT	TRAINED
FEARLESS	VETERAN

ANTI-TANK PLATOON (SP), ROYAL ARTILLERY

PLATOON

4 M10 3" SP	240 points
2 M10 3" SP	120 points
4 M10C 17 pdr SP	260 points
2 M10C17 pdr SP	130 points

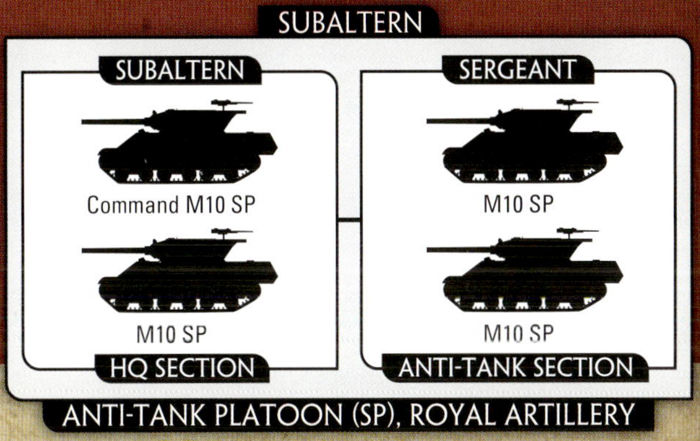

ANTI-TANK PLATOON, ROYAL ARTILLERY

PLATOON

HQ Section with:

4 OQF 6 pdr	100 points
2 OQF 6 pdr	50 points

OPTION

- Add Troop and Loyd Carriers for +5 points for the platoon.

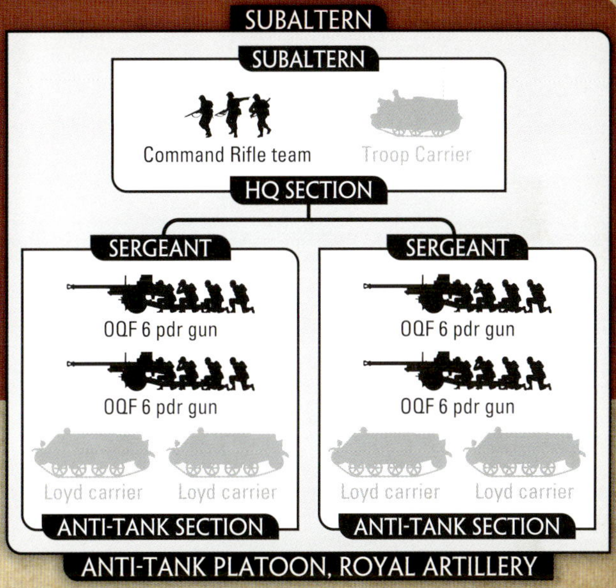

HEAVY ANTI-TANK PLATOON, ROYAL ARTILLERY

PLATOON

HQ Section with:

4 OQF 17 pdr	175 points
2 OQF 17 pdr	85 points

OPTION

- Add M5 half-tracks for +5 points for the platoon.

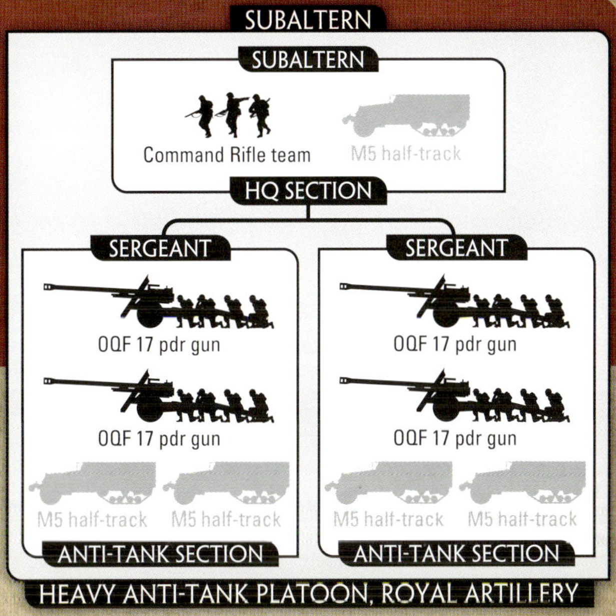

Field Battery, Royal Artillery

Platoon

HQ Troop with:

Two Gun Troops with a total of:

8 OQF 25 pdr	250 points

One Gun Troop with:

4 OQF 25 pdr	145 points
2 OQF 25 pdr	85 points

Options

- Add Jeep, 15 cwt trucks, and Quad tractors for +5 points per Gun Troop.
- Replace the HQ Troop Jeep with a White scout car for +5 points.
- Replace any or all Observer Rifle teams and their OP Carriers with Observer Sherman OP tanks for +10 points per tank.

OQF 25 pdr Gun

Equipment	Notes	Movement
Gun shield, Smoke, Turntable	Smoke bombardment	Heavy

Weapon	Range	ROF	AT	FP
OQF 25 pdr gun	*24"/60cm*	*2*	*9*	*3+*
Firing bombardments	*80"/200cm*	*-*	*4*	*5+*

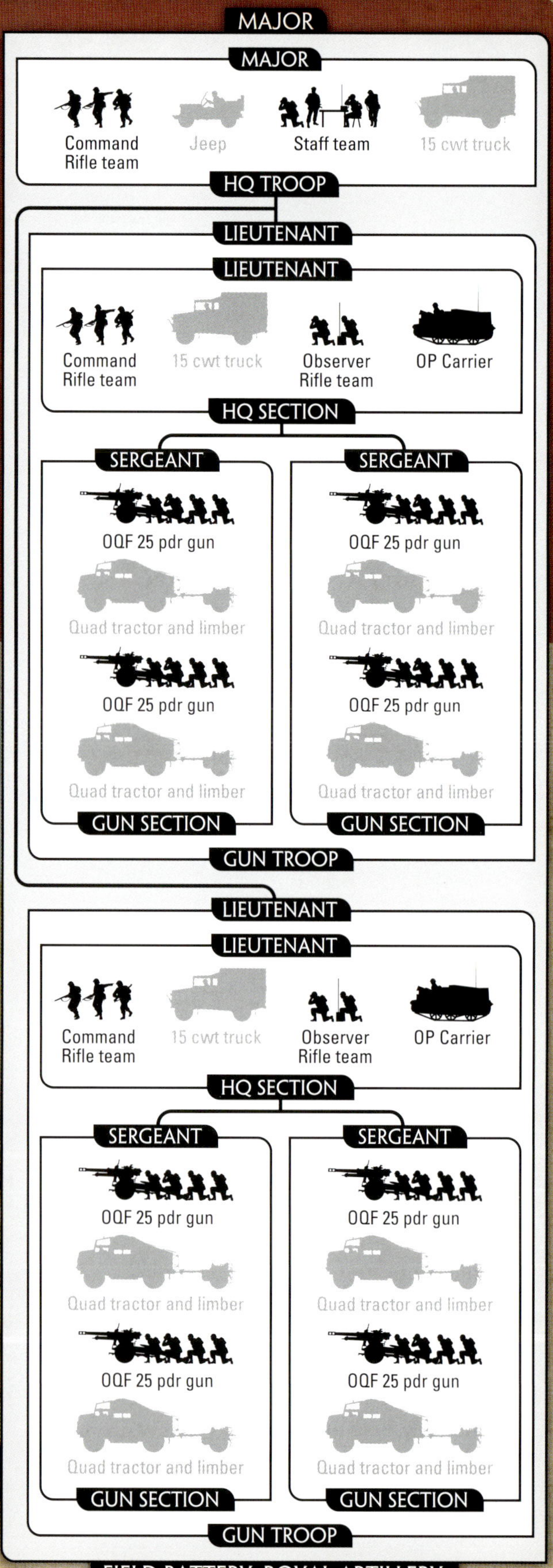

FIELD BATTERY, ROYAL ARTILLERY

Field Battery (SP), Royal Artillery

Platoon

HQ Troop with:

Two Gun Troops with a total of:

8 Sexton	340 points

One Gun Troop with:

4 Sexton	195 points
2 Sexton	110 points

Options

- Add Jeep and 15 cwt trucks for +5 points for the battery.
- Replace the HQ Troop jeep with a White scout car for +5 points.

Sexton

Weapon	Range	ROF	AT	FP	Notes
OQF 25 pdr gun	24"/60cm	2	9	3+	Hull-mounted, Smoke.
Firing bombardments	80"/200cm	-	4	5+	Smoke bombardment.

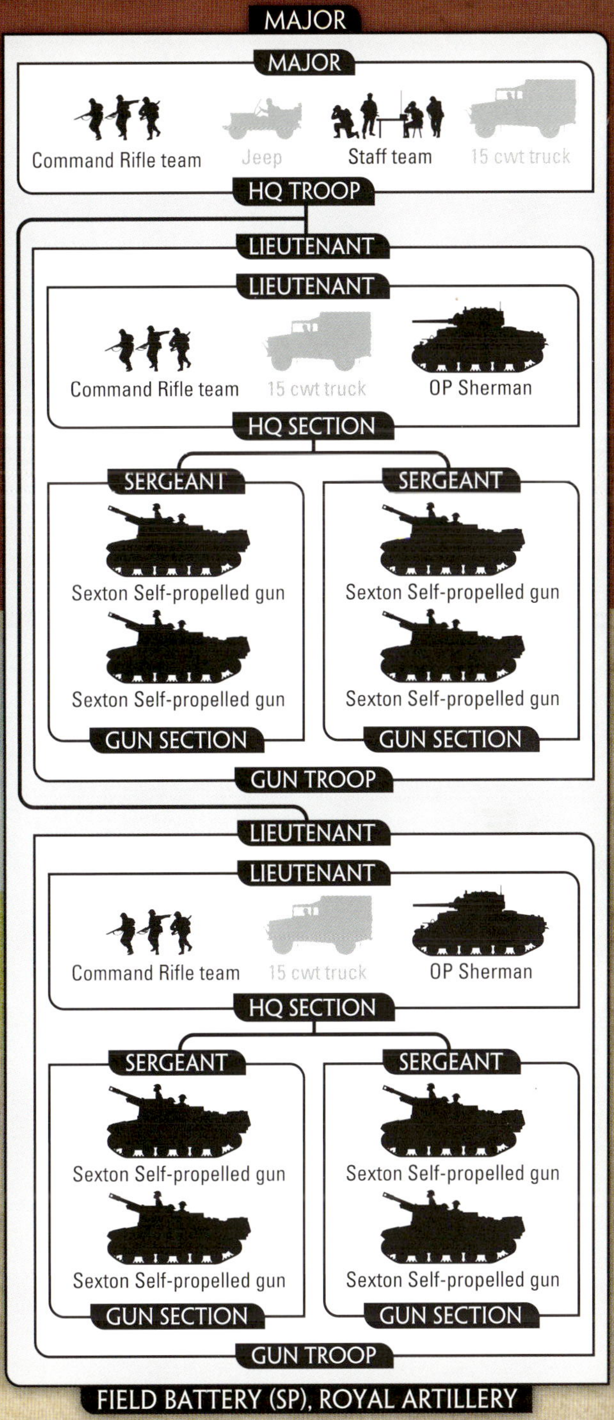

Armoured Car Platoon

Platoon

2 Daimler I and 1 Daimler Dingo	95 points

Options

- Fit Littlejohn adaptor to one Daimler I armoured car at no cost.
- Replace AA MG on Daimler Dingo scout car with .50 cal AA MG for +5 points.

To improve the anti-tank performance of the 2 pdr gun, some were fitted with Littlejohn squeeze-bore adaptors that accelerated sub-calibre shot to a higher velocity and significantly increased its anti-tank capability.

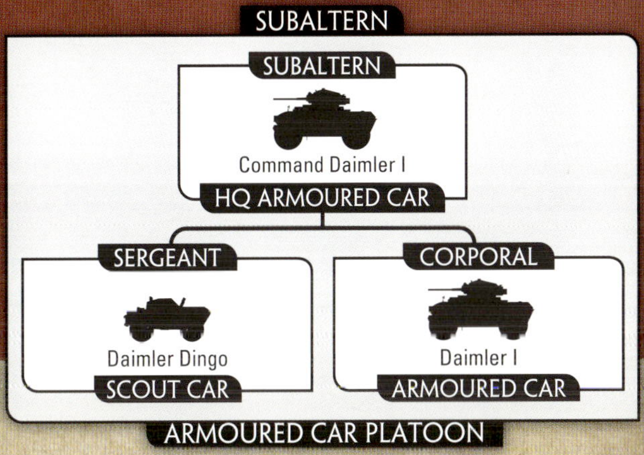

An Armoured Car Platoon is a Reconnaissance Platoon.

Medium Battery, Royal Artillery

Platoon

HQ Troop with:

Two Gun Troops with a total of:

8 BL 5.5”	415 points

One Gun Troop with:

4 BL 5.5”	240 points
2 BL 5.5”	130 points

Option

- Add Jeep, 15 cwt trucks and Matador tractors for +5 points per gun troop.

You may not field a Medium Battery, Royal Artillery unless you are also fielding a Field Battery, Royal Artillery or Field Battery (SP), Royal Artillery with at least as many guns.

BL 5.5” gun

Notes	Movement
Bunker buster	Immobile

Weapon	Range	ROF	AT	FP
BL 5.5” gun	*32”/80cm*	*1*	*13*	*1+*
Firing bombardments	*88”/220cm*	*-*	*5*	*2+*

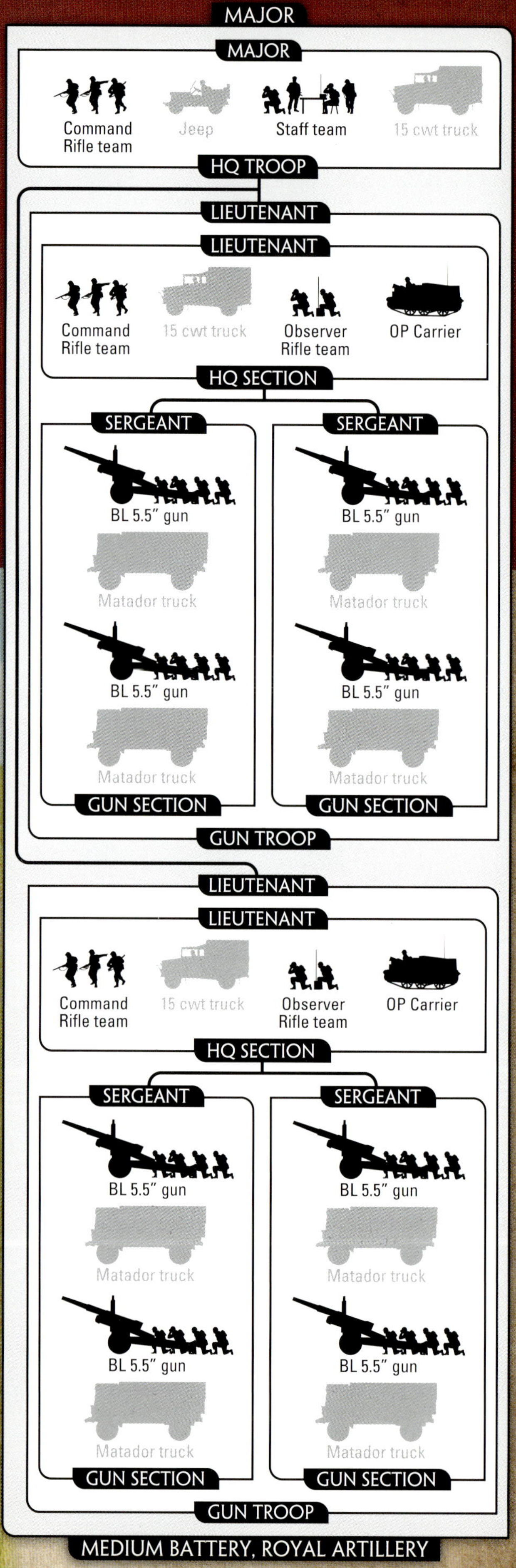

Tank Platoon

Platoon

3 Churchill VI	260 points

Options

- Upgrade any or all Churchill VI tanks with applique armour increasing the Front armour rating to 9 for +10 points per tank.
- Replace Command Churchill VI tank with a Command Churchill VII tank for +45 points.

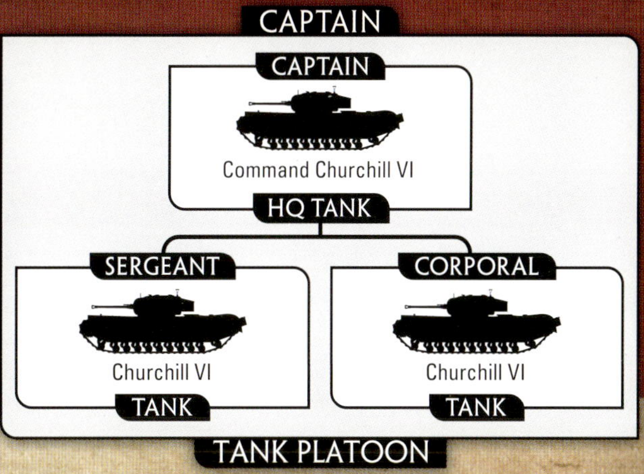

Some Churchill tanks had additional armoured plates welded to vulnerable locations in the form of applique armour to increase their protection against enemy fire.

Churchill VI

Weapon	Range	ROF	AT	FP	Notes
OQF 75mm gun	*32"/80cm*	*2*	*10*	*3+*	*Semi-indirect fire, Smoke.*

Churchill VII

Weapon	Range	ROF	AT	FP	Notes
OQF 75mm gun	*32"/80cm*	*2*	*10*	*3+*	*Semi-indirect fire, Smoke, Slow traverse.*

Air Support

Priority Air Support

Typhoon	220 points

Limited Air Support

Typhoon	170 points

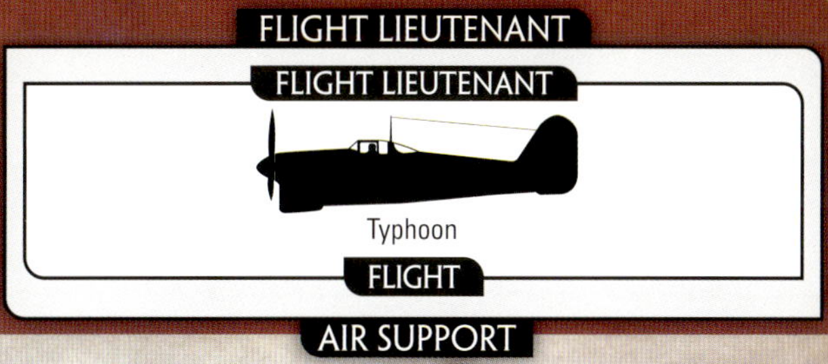

British Arsenal

Tank Teams

Name *Weapon*	Mobility *Range*	Front *ROF*	Armour Side *Anti-tank*	Top *Firepower*	Equipment and Notes
Light Tanks					
Stuart V	Light Tank	4	2	1	Co-ax MG, Hull MG.
M6 37mm gun	*24"/60cm*	*2*	*7*	*4+*	
Stuart V Jalopy	Light Tank	4	2	0	Hull .50 cal MG, Hull MG, Wide tracks.
Medium Tanks					
Sherman V	Standard Tank	6	4	1	Co-ax MG, Hull MG, Tow hook.
M3 75mm gun	*32"/80cm*	*2*	*10*	*3+*	*Semi-indirect fire, Smoke.*
Firefly VC	Standard Tank	6	4	1	Co-ax MG, Tow hook.
OQF 17 pdr gun	*32"/80cm*	*2*	*13*	*3+*	*No HE, Semi-indirect fire.*
Infantry Tanks					
Churchill VI	Slow Tank	8	7	2	Co-ax MG, Hull MG, Protected ammo, Tow hook, Wide tracks.
OQF 75mm gun	*32"/80cm*	*2*	*10*	*3+*	*Semi-indirect fire, Smoke.*
Churchill VII	Slow Tank	13	8	2	Co-ax MG, Hull MG, Protected ammo, Tow hook, Wide tracks.
OQF 75mm gun	*32"/80cm*	*2*	*10*	*3+*	*Semi-indirect fire, Slow traverse, Smoke.*
Self-propelled Anti-tank Guns					
M10 3" SP	Standard Tank	4	2	0	.50 cal AA MG.
M7 3" gun	*32"/80cm*	*2*	*12*	*3+*	*Slow traverse.*
M10C 17 pdr SP	Standard Tank	4	2	0	.50 cal AA MG.
OQF 17 pdr gun	*32"/80cm*	*2*	*13*	*3+*	*No HE, Slow traverse.*
Self-propelled Guns					
Sexton	Standard Tank	1	0	0	AA MG.
OQF 25 pdr gun	*24"/60cm*	*2*	*9*	*3+*	*Hull mounted, Smoke.*
Firing bombardments	*80"/200cm*	*-*	*4*	*5+*	*Smoke bombardment.*
Sherman OP	Standard Tank	6	4	1	Hull MG.
Infantry Support					
Wasp Carrier	Half-tracked	0	0	0	
Wasp flame-gun	*4"/10cm*	*3*	*-*	*6*	*Hull mounted, Flame-thrower.*
Reconnaissance					
Universal Carrier	Half-tracked	0	0	0	Hull MG.
With PIAT anti-tank projector	*8"/20cm*	*1*	*10*	*5+*	*Hull-mounted*
With .50 cal MG	*16"/40cm*	*3*	*4*	*5+*	*Hull-mounted*
Daimler Dingo	Jeep	1	0	0	AA MG.
Daimler I	Wheeled	1	0	0	Co-ax MG.
OQF 2 pdr gun	*24"/60cm*	*2*	*7*	*4+*	
With Littlejohn adaptor	*24"/60cm*	*2*	*9*	*5+*	*No HE.*
Vehicle Machine-guns					
Vehicle MG	*16"/40cm*	*3*	*2*	*6*	*ROF 1 if other weapons fire.*
.50 cal Vehicle MG	*16"/40cm*	*3*	*4*	*5+*	*ROF 1 if other weapons fire.*

GUN TEAMS

Weapon	Mobility	Range	ROF	Anti-tank	Firepower	Notes
Vickers HMG	Man-packed	24"/60cm	6	2	6	ROF 3 when pinned down or moving.
Firing bombardments		40"/100cm	-	-	-	
Vickers (Motor) HMG	Man-packed	24"/60cm	6	2	6	ROF 3 when pinned down or moving.
ML 3" Mk II mortar	Man-packed	24"/60cm	2	2	3+	Smoke, Minimum range 8"/20cm.
Firing bombardments		40"/100cm	-	2	6	Smoke bombardment.
ML 4.2" mortar	Light	48"/120cm	-	3	4+	Smoke bombardment.
OQF 6 pdr gun	Medium	24"/60cm	3	10	4+	Gun shield.
OQF 17 pdr gun	Immobile	32"/80cm	2	13	3+	Gun shield, No HE.
OQF 25 pdr gun	Heavy	24"/60cm	2	9	3+	Gun shield, Smoke, Turntable.
Firing bombardments		80"/200cm	-	4	5+	Smoke bombardment.
BL 5.5" gun	Immobile	32"/80cm	1	13	1+	Bunker buster.
Firing bombardments		88"/220cm	-	5	2+	

INFANTRY TEAMS

Team	Range	ROF	Anti-tank	Firepower	Notes
Rifle team	16"/40cm	1	2	6	
Rifle/MG team	16"/40cm	2	2	6	
MG team	16"/40cm	3	2	6	ROF 2 when pinned down.
Light Mortar team	16"/40cm	1	1	4+	Smoke, Can fire over friendly teams.
PIAT team	8"/20cm	1	10	5+	Tank Assault 4.
Observer Rifle team	16"/40cm	1	2	6	Observer
Staff team			cannot shoot		Moves as a Heavy Gun team.

TRANSPORT TEAMS

Vehicle	Mobility	Armour Front	Armour Side	Armour Top	Equipment and Notes
TRUCKS					
Jeep	Jeep	-	-	-	
Morris or Chev 15 cwt truck	Wheeled	-	-	-	
Quad or Matador Tractor	Wheeled	-	-	-	
TROOP CARRIERS					
White scout car	Jeep	1	0	0	
M5 half-track	Half-tracked	1	0	0	
Troop, OP, Mortar, or Loyd Carrier	Half-tracked	0	0	0	
MMG Carrier	Half-tracked	0	0	0	HMG Carrier, Passenger-fired hull MG.

AIRCRAFT

Aircraft	Weapon	To Hit	Anti-tank	Firepower	Notes
Typhoon	Cannon	3+	8	5+	
	Rockets	3+	6	3+	

The Typhoon was designed as a replacement for the famous Hawker Hurricane in the bomber interceptor role, but failed to deliver the high-altitude performance needed in that role. What it had instead was stunning low-level performance and a rugged airframe making it an excellent fighter-bomber.

Each Typhoon carries eight 60lb (27kg) HE rockets. Against most targets the rockets are the preferred weapon. Rockets are more accurate than bombs and much more deadly than the fire of the Typhoon's four 20mm cannon.

8 x 60lb rockets (112lb/51kg of explosives per aircraft)

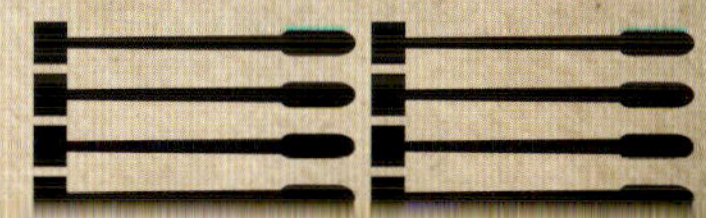

SOVIET FORCES, 1944

Comrades! Our forces are numberless. The over-weening enemy will soon learn this to his cost. Side by side with the Red Army many thousands of workers, collective farmers and intellectuals are rising to fight the enemy aggressor. The masses of the people will rise up in their millions.

—Iosef Stalin

Comrade soldiers! Today we fight for the very survival of International Communism and for the soul of the Motherland. The long struggle for the freedom of the workers and peasants continues as the RKKA, our glorious Workers' and Peasants' Red Army, smashes the fascist hordes, annihilating them where they stand and pursuing them to the viper's nest from whence they came!

It was only the treason of the old Tsarist officers and the cowardice of the men they led that opened the door letting the Hitlerites invade your beloved homeland. Their backstab cost the people of the Soviet Union dearly, bringing the enemy to the very gates of Moscow and Stalingrad, and our glorious Soviet Union to the brink of defeat.

Fortunately our beloved leader, Comrade Stalin, stood strong, purging the traitors and, with his 'Not One Step Back' order, putting steel in the backbone of the army.

Comrade soldiers! Despite the unbending steel of Comrade Stalin's leadership, the war is not yet won. It is your duty, your honour, your glory, to lead us to victory. Yesterday you worked in the factories of the Urals, in the fields of Kazakstan, and in the icy wastes of Siberia. Today you are soldiers. Tomorrow you will fight.

Some of you are riflemen, the lifeblood of the Red Army. Like the Volga in spring, you will be irresistible. As you march unflinchingly into the fire of the fascist vipers and defeat them, your flood will wash away the stain left by the fascist beast on our beloved Motherland.

Brave comrades! Always remember that the very future of workers throughout the world depends on you. Do not falter in your steps. Do not fear treason. Your comrade komissar stands ready to eliminate traitors the moment they show themselves. Do your duty as a hero selflessly. Do not hesitate. Do not allow yourself even one step back!

Nothing must be allowed to get in the way of victory—neither the futile resistance of the enemy nor any selfish thoughts regarding personal survival. Indeed, the life of the individual is meaningless when set against the survival of Mother Russia and the glorious Communist system.

You will not fight alone. The entire might of the Red Army will fight with you. Our tankists will lead the way, our artillerists will flatten the enemy defences ahead of you, while our Shturmoviki pound them from the air.

Others of you are those tankists. Your tanks are more than a match for any puny fascist panzer. The workers of the Soviet Union have sweated blood to bring you these machines. Do not waste their effort.

With many of our factories overrun by the Hitlerites, the world thought we were doomed. They did not count on

the resilience of the Soviet worker. Racing the advancing panzers, they dismantled their factories and rebuilt them in the Urals. Standing in the snow they built tanks before they built factories, or even houses to live in. Workers toil twenty-four hours a day to produce the advanced weaponry conceived by our brilliant Soviet engineers.

Tomorrow when you fight, you must remember all you have learned in your training. Destroy the Fascists. Let not one survive, and if your tank is hit, do not hesitate, fight on. Strike back and destroy the gun that shot you. Do not abandon your tank while it can still fight. Push deep into the enemy positions and do not stop while you have breath, fuel and ammunition.

The cavalry of the Red Army will be thundering alongside you upon hooves of fury. Many of these brave comrades are from that race of renowned horse warriors the Cossacks. In the solidarity of the Communist Brotherhood, they too resist the Nazi invaders.

And let us not forget the artillerists. Their powerful guns are the 'Red God of War'. Their numberless guns will blast a path into the Hitlerite lines for you. Our Soviet system is simple, direct and effective. We do not waste precious ammunition throwing shells at the enemy like a Tsar scattering roubles at a festival. We mass our guns where they are needed, where they can see the enemy, where they can make every shot count. Nothing can stand up to a full artillery battalion! Nothing will stop you achieving victory!

Comrade soldiers! We are ridding the soil of the Rodina of the Nazi pestilence. Through your selfless sacrifice we will prevail over the low cunning of the fascist generals and their arrogant hordes.

Tomorrow we march to victory. Tomorrow we fight. Tomorrow the fascists die. Tomorrow will be a glorious day for the Motherland!

Each day brings us closer to ultimate victory comrades. Yes, the day will come when our soldiers parade Hitler himself in chains across Red Square!

TANKOVY BATALON

(TANK BATTALION)

RELUCTANT	CONSCRIPT
CONFIDENT	**TRAINED**
FEARLESS	VETERAN

TANK COMPANY

HEADQUARTERS

HEADQUARTERS

- HEADQUARTERS: Company Command tank — Tankovy Batalon HQ

COMBAT COMPANIES

- ARMOUR: Tankovy Company 79
- ARMOUR: Tankovy Company 79
- ARMOUR: Light Tankovy Company 85

WEAPONS COMPANIES

- ANTI-TANK: Tank Destruction Company 97
- INFANTRY: Motostrelkovy Company 81
- ARTILLERY: Motostrelkovy Mortar Company 82

DIVISIONAL SUPPORT COMPANIES

- ARMOUR: Guards Heavy Tank Company 92
- ARMOUR: Guards Heavy Assault Gun Company 93; Assault Gun Company 91; Tank Killer Company 94
- ARMOUR: Assault Gun Company 91; Tank Killer Company 94; Tank Destruction Company 97
- INFANTRY: Motostrelkovy Company 81
- INFANTRY: Sapper Company 94
- ARTILLERY: Heavy Mortar Company 83
- ARTILLERY: Guards Rocket Mortar Battalion 97
- AIRCRAFT: Air Support 91

HEADQUARTERS

Company HQ with:

T-34 obr 1942	55 points
T-34/85 obr 1943	80 points

- Upgrade T-34 obr 1942 or T-34/85 obr 1943 tank to have a cupola for +5 points.
- Mount a SMG Tank Escort on the Company Command tank for +10 points.

For sheer brute force, nothing beats a Tankovy Batalon or tank battalion. This is really a heavy-metal force with twenty or even thirty good tanks. Of course, when fielding such a large force coordination is difficult, so you have to keep your tactics simple. Keep the enemy in sight and blow them away with massed firepower or overwhelm them in close-range combat!

COMBAT COMPANIES

TANKOVY COMPANY

COMPANY

10 T-34 obr 1942	450 points
9 T-34 obr 1942	420 points
8 T-34 obr 1942	390 points
7 T-34 obr 1942	355 points
6 T-34 obr 1942	320 points
5 T-34 obr 1942	275 points

OPTIONS

- Replace up to five T-34 obr 1942 tanks with T-34/85 obr 1943 tanks for +25 points per tank.
- Upgrade all T-34 obr 1942 and T-34/85 obr 1943 tanks to have Cupolas for +10 points for the company.
- Mount SMG Tank Escorts on all tanks for +10 points per tank.

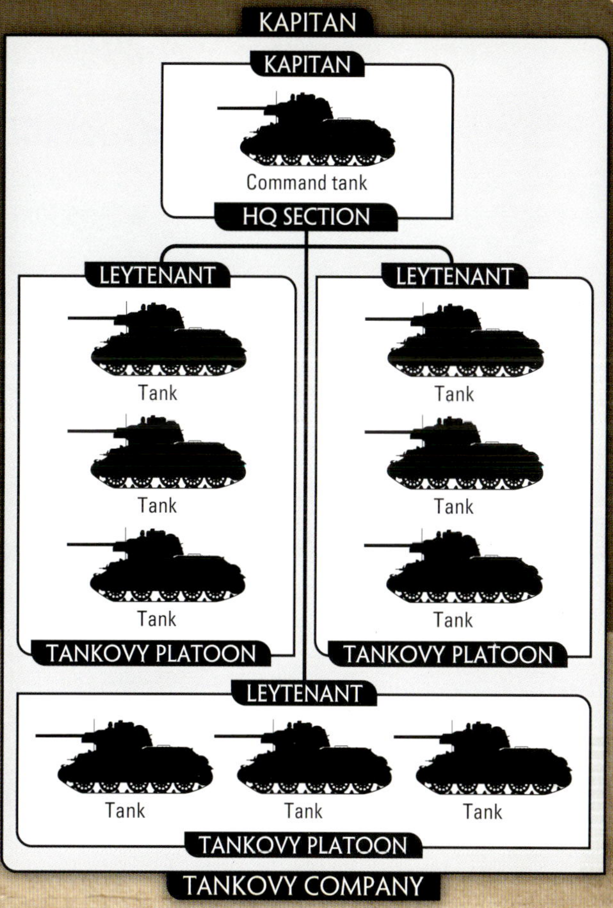

CUPOLAS

During 1943 new T-34 tanks were fitted with a commander's cupola, a raised hatch that allows the commander to keep an eye on the developing battle outside through vision slits in the cupola's sides. In *Flames Of War* Soviet Tanks fitted with a commander's cupola no longer have limited vision, so do not suffer any penalty for shooting to the flanks (see pages 118 and 252 of the *Flames Of War* rulebook).

T-34 OBR 1942

Armament: 76mm F-34 gun, Co-ax MG, Hull MG, Limited vision

Top Armour: 1

Front Armour: 6 | **Movement:** Standard Tank, Fast tank, Wide-tracks. | **Side Armour:** 5

Weapon	Range	ROF	AT	FP	Notes
76mm F-34 gun	32"/80cm	2	9	3+	

T-34/85 OBR 1943

Armament: 85mm D-5T gun, Co-ax MG, Hull MG, Limited vision

Top Armour: 1

Side Armour: 5 | **Movement:** Standard tank | **Front Armour:** 7

Weapon	Range	ROF	AT	FP	Notes
85mm D-5T gun	32"/80cm	2	12	3+	

HEN AND CHICKS

Soviet tank losses were incredible. In 1942, they built 10,000 light tanks, 12,000 medium tanks, and 2,000 heavy tanks, and received 4,500 more from Britain, Canada, and America. In that year they lost 16,000 of them, far more tanks than any other army even possessed! The only way the Red Army could keep up with such losses was to rush tank crews into battle with minimal training. Combined with a lack of radios and a preference for going into battle with all hatches closed, this resulted in Soviet tanks blindly following their company commander, as the Germans described it 'like chicks following the mother hen'.

In *Flames Of War* if a Soviet Platoon Command team moves in the Movement Step, all of the Tank and Transport teams in its platoon (Soviet company) must move as well. In addition if you decide to shoot any of your Soviet vehicles on the move they suffer an additional +1 to the score required to hit when shooting with their main guns. Machine-guns and Flame-throwers do not suffer this penalty (see page 252 of the *Flames Of War* rulebook).

However, Soviet do come in very large units when compared to their allies and enemies, so their massed firepower will often off set their disadvantage in tactical training.

MOTOSTRELKOVY BATALON

(MOTOR RIFLE BATTALION)

RELUCTANT | CONSCRIPT
CONFIDENT | TRAINED
FEARLESS | VETERAN

MECHANISED COMPANY

HEADQUARTERS

Battalion HQ	30 points

The Motostrelkovy Batalon or motor-rifle battalion comes with a core of well-equipped infantry backed up with every imaginable form of support weaponry, and plenty of room for lots of tanks too. This is the ultimate combined-arms force.

HEADQUARTERS

HEADQUARTERS
- Company Command Rifle team
- 2iC Command Rifle team
- Battalion Komissar team

Motostrelkovy Batalon HQ

COMBAT COMPANIES

- INFANTRY — Motostrelkovy Company 81
- INFANTRY — Motostrelkovy Company 81
- INFANTRY — Motostrelkovy Company 81
- ARTILLERY — Motostrelkovy Mortar Company 82
- MACHINE-GUNS — Motostrelkovy Machine-gun Company 81
- ANTI-TANK — Motostrelkovy Anti-tank Company 82

WEAPONS COMPANIES

- ARMOUR — Tankovy Company 79 / Light Tankovy Company 85
- ARTILLERY — Motostrelkovy Mortar Company 82
- ARTILLERY — Heavy Mortar Company 83
- INFANTRY — Submachine-gun Company 83
- ARTILLERY — Motostrelkovy Artillery Battalion 84
- INFANTRY — Sapper Company 94

DIVISIONAL SUPPORT COMPANIES

- ARMOUR — Tankovy Company 79 / Light Tankovy Company 85
- ARMOUR — Guards Heavy Tank Company 92
- ARMOUR — Guards Heavy Assault Gun Company 93 / Assault Gun Company 91 / Tank Killer Company 94
- ARMOUR — Assault Gun Company 91 / Tank Killer Company 94 / Tank Destruction Company 97
- ANTI-TANK — Tank Destruction Company 97
- ARTILLERY — Reserve Heavy Artillery Battalion 96
- ARTILLERY — Guards Rocket Mortar Battalion 97
- AIRCRAFT — Air Support 91

COMBAT COMPANIES

MOTOSTRELKOVY COMPANY

COMPANY

HQ Section with:

3 Motor Rifle Platoons	350 points
2 Motor Rifle Platoons	240 points
1 Motor Rifle Platoon	130 points

OPTIONS

- Add Komissar team for +15 points.
- Add Maksim HMG teams for +25 points per team.

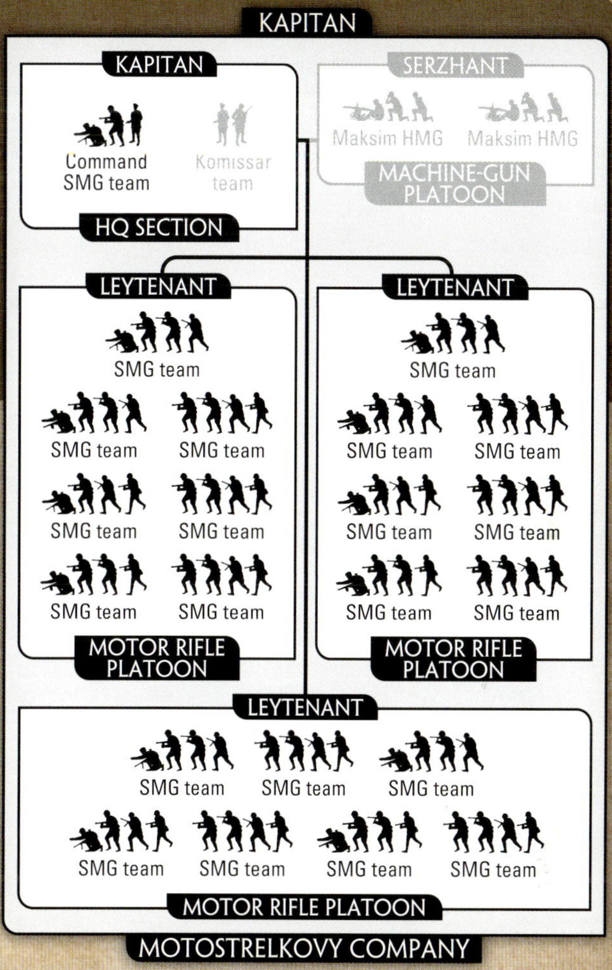

THE SMG AND ASSAULTS

The Motostrelkovy Company operates with the tanks and engages in short range fighting in support of the tanks. The PPSh-41 submachine-gun the ideal weapon for short range firefights. In *Flames Of War* this make them particularly useful preparing for assaults.

A SMG team has a ROF 3, even when moving, which allows the Motostrelkovy Company, with up to 22 such teams or 66 dice, to pump out a lot of shots in the Shooting Step before you launch an assault. Often a Motostrelkovy Company can simply Pin Down an enemy platoon with this one step of shooting. This ability to mass a short heavy burst of shooting makes them ideal assault troops. However, remember that SMG teams only have a shooting range of 4"/10cm, so make sure they are not exposed during their approach to too much enemy long range fire.

MOTOSTRELKOVY MACHINE-GUN COMPANY

COMPANY

HQ Section with:

9 Maksim HMG	220 points
6 Maksim HMG	150 points
3 Maksim HMG	80 points

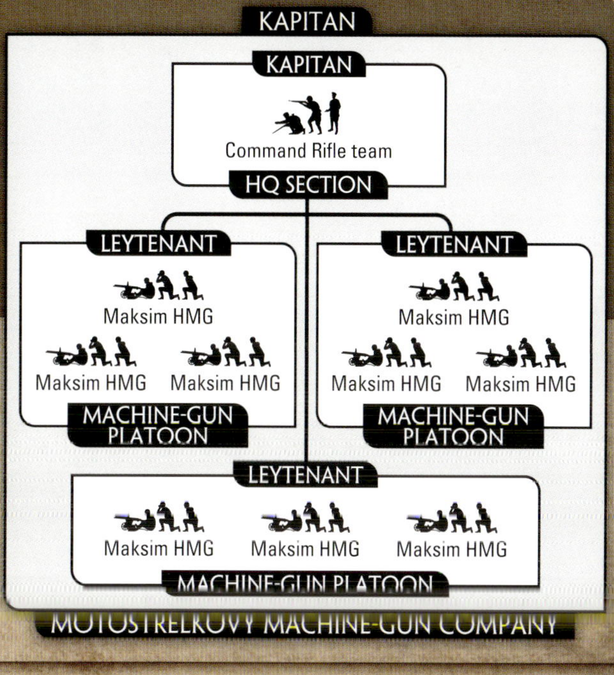

PPSH-41 submachine-gun

Motostrelkovy Mortar Company

Company

HQ Section with:

6 82-BM-41	95 points
3 82-BM-41	60 points

Options

- Add trucks for +5 for the company.
- Add Observer Rifle team for +15 points.

Weapon	Range	ROF	AT	FP
82-BM-41 mortar	24"/60cm	2	2	3+
Firing bombardments	40"/100cm	-	2	6

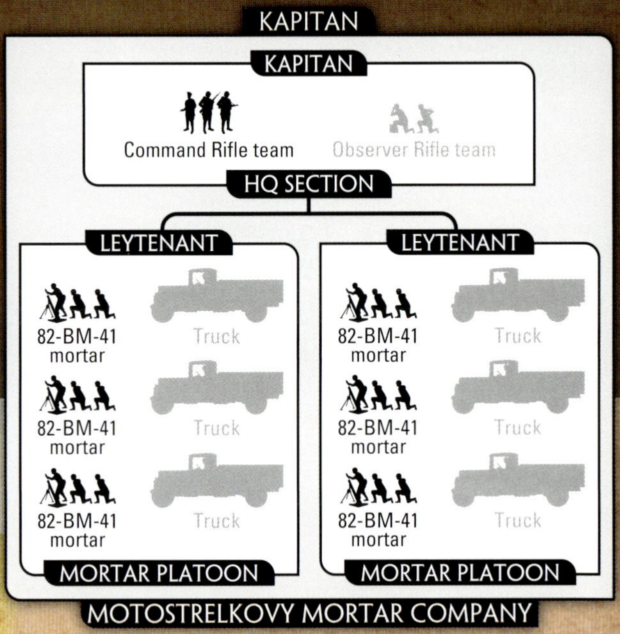

Motostrelkovy Anti-tank Company

Company

HQ Section with:

4 45mm obr 1942	85 points
2 45mm obr 1942	45 points

Option

- Add trucks for +5 for the company.

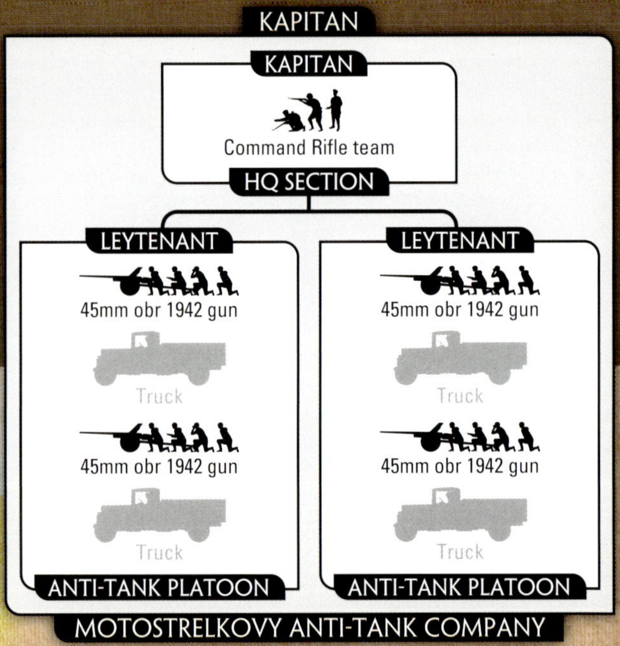

Weapon	Range	ROF	AT	FP
45mm obr 1942 gun	24"/60cm	3	8	4+

WEAPONS COMPANIES

HEAVY MORTAR COMPANY

COMPANY

HQ Section with:

6 120-PM-38	130 points
4 120-PM-38	95 points

OPTIONS

- Add trucks for +5 for the company.
- Add Observer Rifle team for +15 points.

Weapon	Range	ROF	AT	FP
120-PM-38 mortar	56"/140cm	-	3	3+

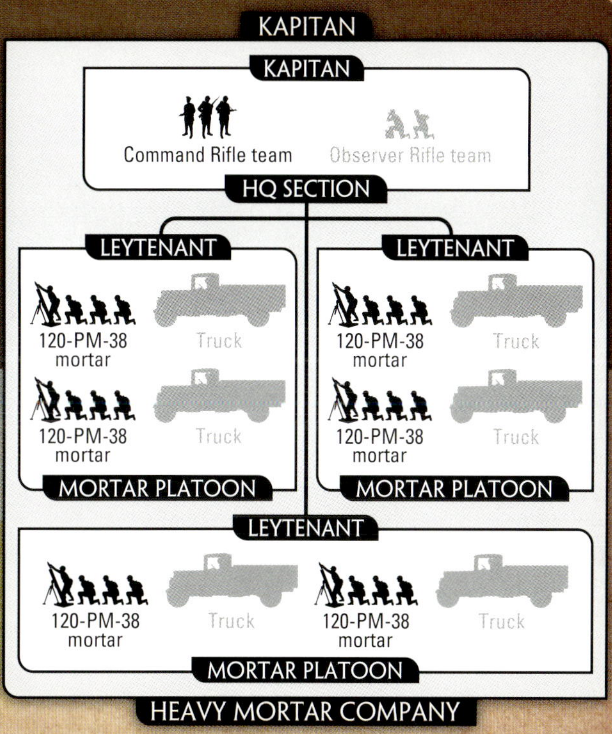

SUBMACHINE-GUN COMPANY

COMPANY

HQ Section with:

3 Submachine-gun Platoons	350 points
2 Submachine-gun Platoons	240 points
1 Submachine-gun Platoon	130 points

OPTION

- Add Komissar team for +15 points.

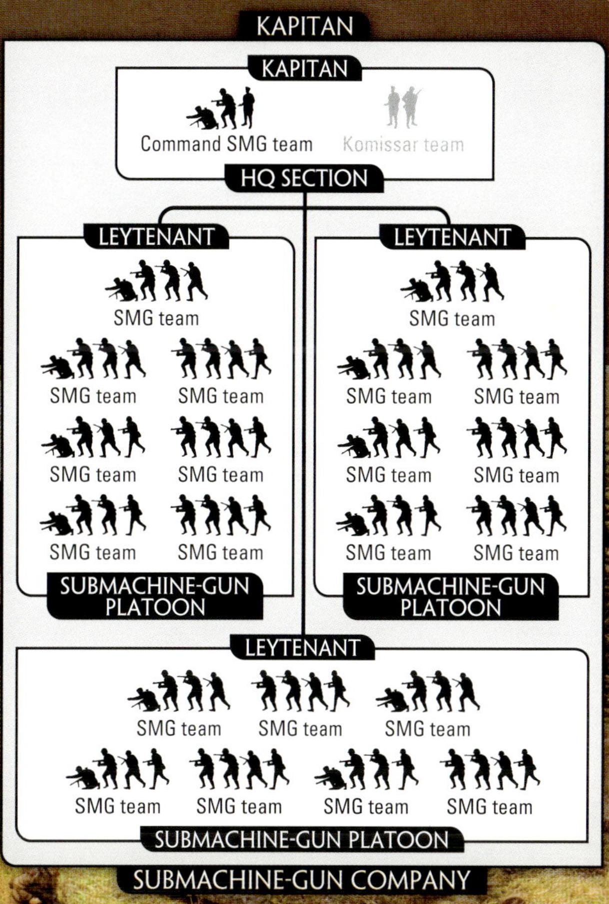

Motostrelkovy Artillery Battalion

Company

HQ Section with:

12 76mm ZIS-3 field gun	235 points
8 76mm ZIS-3 field gun	190 points
4 76mm ZIS-3 field gun	115 points

Options

- Add Observer team for +15 points.
- Add trucks for +5 points for the battalion.

76mm ZIS-3 Field Gun

Equipment	Movement
Gun shield	Heavy

Weapon	Range	ROF	AT	FP
76mm ZIS-3 field gun	32"/80cm	2	9	3+
Firing bombardments	80"/200cm	-	3	6

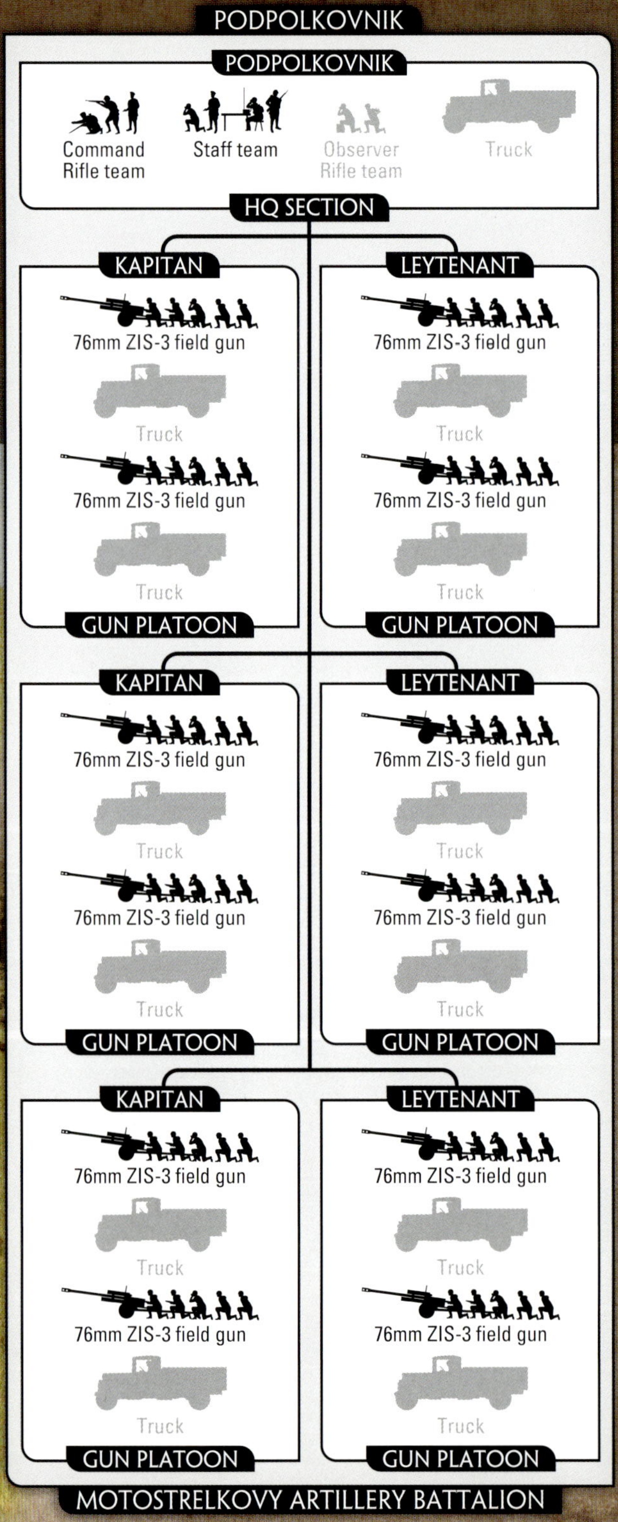

LIGHT TANKOVY COMPANY

COMPANY

10 T-70 obr 1943	200 points
9 T-70 obr 1943	190 points
8 T-70 obr 1943	175 points
7 T-70 obr 1943	160 points
6 T-70 obr 1943	145 points
5 T-70 obr 1943	120 points
10 Mark III (Valentine II)	265 points
9 Mark III (Valentine II)	250 points
8 Mark III (Valentine II)	230 points
7 Mark III (Valentine II)	210 points
6 Mark III (Valentine II)	185 points
5 Mark III (Valentine II)	160 points

- Replace any or all Mark III (Valentine II) tanks with Mark III (Valentine VIII) tanks at no cost.

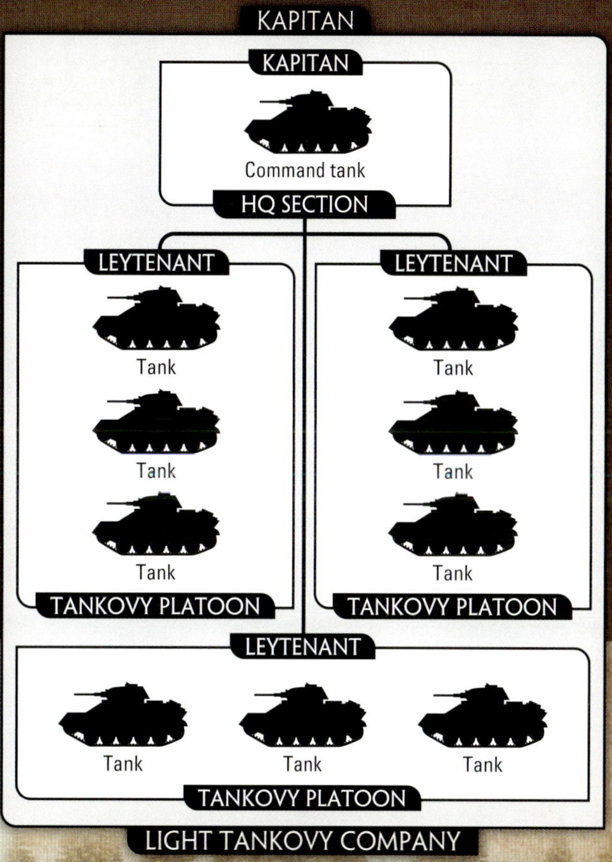

T-70 OBR 1943

Weapon	Range	ROF	AT	FP	Notes
45mm obr 1943 gun	24"/60cm	1	7	4+	

MARK III (VALENTINE II)

Weapon	Range	ROF	AT	FP	Notes
OQF 2 pdr gun	24"/60cm	2	7	4+	

MARK III (VALENTINE VIII)

Weapon	Range	ROF	AT	FP	Notes
OQF 6 pdr gun	24"/60cm	2	10	4+	

STRELKOVY BATALON

(RIFLE BATTALION)

RELUCTANT	CONSCRIPT
CONFIDENT	TRAINED
FEARLESS	VETERAN

INFANTRY COMPANY

HEADQUARTERS

HEADQUARTERS

- Company Command Rifle team
- 2iC Command Rifle team
- Battalion Komissar team

Strelkovy Batalon HQ

HEADQUARTERS

Battalion HQ	30 points

OPTION

- Add up to three Sniper teams for +50 points per team.

HEADQUARTERS

- Anti-tank Rifle Platoon 87
- Anti-tank Platoon 87
- Sapper Platoon 87

COMBAT COMPANIES

- INFANTRY — Strelkovy Company 88
- INFANTRY — Strelkovy Company 88
- INFANTRY — Strelkovy Company 88
- MACHINE-GUNS — Strelkovy Machine-Gun Company 88
- ARTILLERY — Strelkovy Mortar Company 89

WEAPONS COMPANIES

- ARTILLERY — Heavy Mortar Company 83
- INFANTRY — Submachine-gun Company 83
- RECONNAISSANCE — Strelkovy Scout Platoon 89
- ANTI-TANK OR ARTILLERY — Strelkovy Gun Company 90

DIVISIONAL SUPPORT COMPANIES

- ARMOUR
  - Tankovy Company 79
  - Light Tankovy Company 85
  - Guards Heavy Tank Company 92
- ARMOUR
  - Guards Heavy Assault Gun Company 93
  - Assault Gun Company 91
  - Tank Killer Company 94
- ARMOUR
  - Assault Gun Company 91
  - Tank Killer Company 94
- ANTI-TANK — Tank Destruction Company 97
- INFANTRY — Shtraf Company 90
- INFANTRY — Flame-thrower Platoon 89
- INFANTRY — Sapper Company 94
- ARTILLERY — Artillery Battalion 95
- ARTILLERY — Reserve Heavy Artillery Battalion 96
- ARTILLERY — Guards Rocket Mortar Battalion 97
- AIRCRAFT — Air Support 91

QUALITY OF QUANTITY

The Russians have a saying that 'quantity has a quality all of its own.' The big formations used by the Red Army take a lot of shooting to stop. In *Flames Of War* a platoon (Soviet company) with at least fifteen Infantry or Gun teams must take at least ten hits (instead of the usual five) in a single Shooting Step before they become Pinned Down (see page 251 of the *Flames Of War* rulebook).

The basic building block of the Red Army is the Strelkovy Batalon, the rifle battalion. The essence of this force is a mass of infantry, far more infantry than any other army can field. Your infantry is well supported by a complete range of weapons: machine-guns, mortars, anti-tank guns, tanks, artillery, anti-aircraft guns, and sappers (pioneers).

HEADQUARTERS

The Headquarters Anti-tank Rifle Platoon, Headquarters Anti-tank Platoon, and Headquarters Sapper Platoon are HQ Support Weapons (see page 260 of the Flames Of War rulebook). If not attached out to Combat or Weapons Platoons, teams from these platoon are grouped together as one platoon with the 2iC Command Rifle team as their Platoon Command team.

HEADQUARTERS ANTI-TANK RIFLE PLATOON

Anti-tank Rifle Platoon	40 points

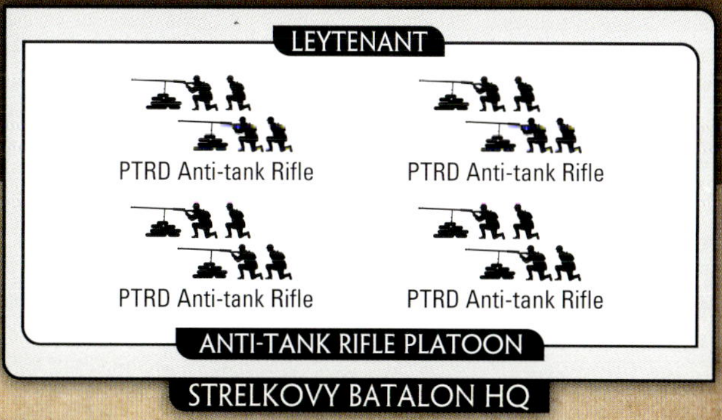

HEADQUARTERS ANTI-TANK PLATOON

Anti-tank Platoon	45 points

HEADQUARTERS SAPPER PLATOON

Sapper Platoon	85 points

OPTION

- Equip Sapper Platoon with a Pioneer Supply wagon for +20 points.

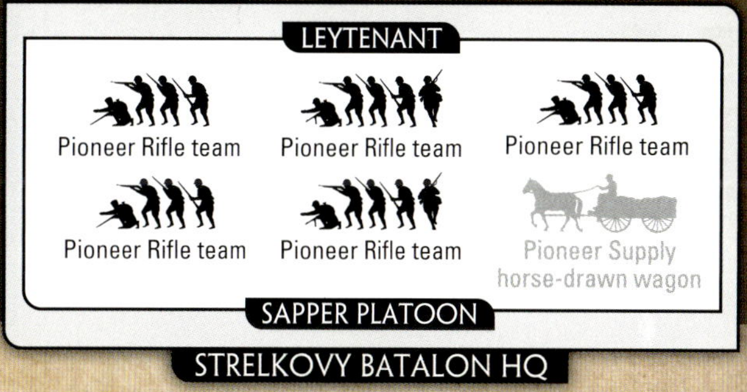

SOVIET WEAPON FIREPOWER

Weapon	Volume of fire (0m–500m)	Weight	Rate of Fire	Magazine	Range
PPSh-41submachine-gun		8lb/4kg	900 rpm	Drum (71) or Box (35)	50m
DP machine-gun		20.5lb/9.2kg	550 rpm	Drum (47)	500m
Mosin-Nagant M1891/30 Rifle		8.7lb/4kg	50 rpm	Clip (5)	500m
Maksim heavy machine-gun		141.7lb/22.2kg	600 rpm	Belt (250)	500m

COMBAT COMPANIES

STRELKOVY COMPANY

COMPANY

HQ Section with:

3 Rifle Platoons	350 points
2 Rifle Platoons	240 points
1 Rifle Platoon	130 points

OPTIONS

- Add Komissar team for +15 points.
- Add Maksim HMG team for +25 points.
- Replace all Rifle/MG teams with SMG teams in one Rifle Platoon at no cost.

INFILTRATION

Soviet soldiers have a reputation for being long-suffering and tough-minded. They swim freezing rivers and wade through trackless swamps in the pitch darkness to reach positions close to, or even behind, the enemy before the battle begins.

The Infiltration special rule (see page 250 of the *Flames Of War* rulebook) allows you to use your Scout Platoon to guide Strelkovy or Submachine-gun Company into No Man's Land ready to start the battle up to 16"/40cm closer to the enemy.

STRELKOVY MACHINE-GUN COMPANY

COMPANY

HQ Section with:

6 Maksim	150 points
3 Maksim	80 points

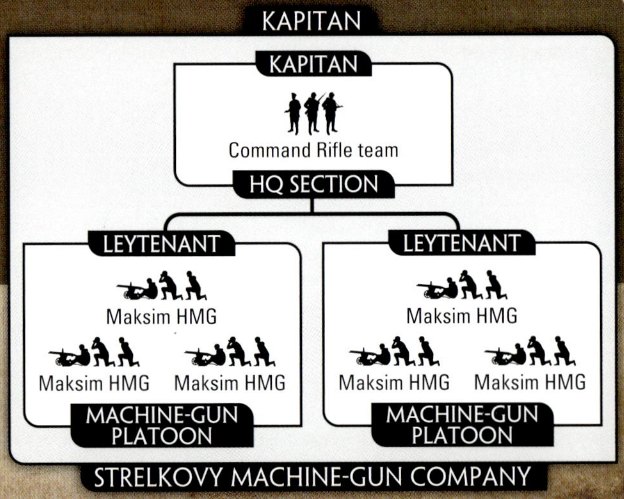

STRELKOVY MORTAR COMPANY

COMPANY

HQ Section with:

6 82-BM-41	95 points
3 82-BM-41	60 points

OPTION

- Add Observer Rifle team for +15 points.

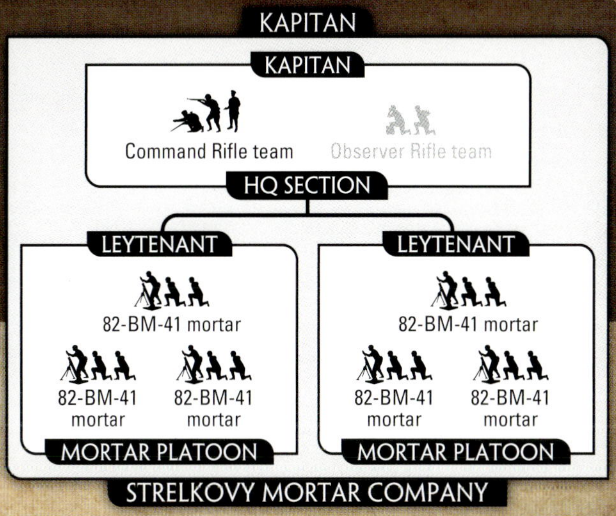

WEAPONS COMPANIES

STRELKOVY SCOUT PLATOON

PLATOON

HQ Section with:

2 Scout Squads	165 points
1 Scout Squad	100 points

Scout Platoons are an exception to the Centralised Control special rule. They operate as a normal platoon.

A Scout Platoon is a Reconnaissance Platoon.

A Scout Platoon is rated as **Fearless Veteran.**

RELUCTANT	CONSCRIPT
CONFIDENT	TRAINED
FEARLESS	**VETERAN**

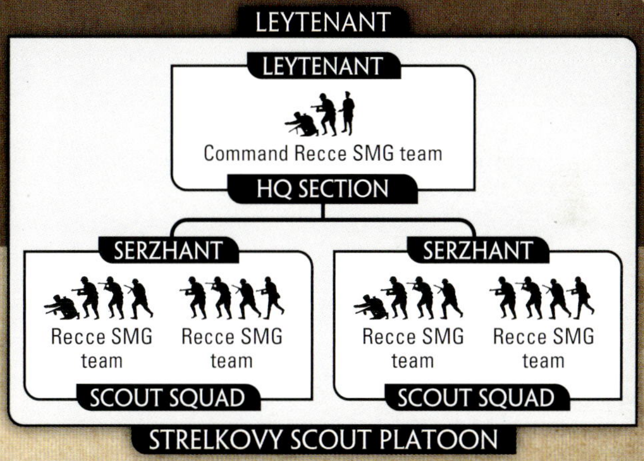

A Scout Platoon is an Infiltration Platoon. They may Infiltrate a Strelkovy Company or Submachine-gun Company, see the Infiltration rules on page 250 of the Flames Of War rulebook.

FLAME-THROWER PLATOON

PLATOON

4 Flame-thrower Sections	360 points
3 Flame-thrower Sections	270 points
2 Flame-thrower Sections	180 points
1 Flame-thrower Section	90 points

Flame-thrower Platoons must make Combat Attachments to Strelkovy Companies and Submachine-gun Companies with all of their sections (see page 260 of the rulebook).

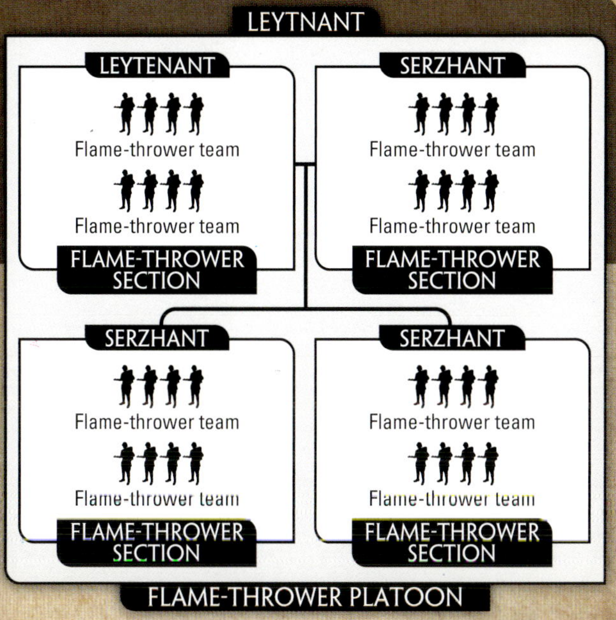

INFANTRY FLAME-THROWERS

The Red Army used infantry flame-throwers with great enthusiasm. Unlike many nations who had just one flame-thrower in a team, the Soviets issued multiple weapons to their teams. This gives the Soviet Flame-thrower teams a high ROF. However, each flame-thrower only has limited fuel, so once they have fired they are removed from play (see pages 198 to 199 of the *Flames Of War* rulebook).

Strelkovy Gun Company

Company

HQ Section with:

4 76mm obr 1927	75 points
2 76mm obr 1927	40 points

- Add Observer Rifle team for +15 points.

HQ Section with:

6 45mm obr 1942	125 points
4 45mm obr 1942	85 points
2 45mm obr 1942	45 points

Option

- Add horse-drawn limbers at +5 points for the company.

Support Companies

Shtraf Company

Company

HQ Section with:

3 Shtraf Platoons	335 points
2 Shtraf Platoons	230 points
1 Shtraf Platoon	125 points

A force fielding a Shtraf Company uses the Shtraf Companies special rule on page 251 of the Flames Of War rulebook.

Soldiers were sent to serve in a Shtraf Company because of failure on the battlefield. As such they are always rated **Fearless Conscript.**

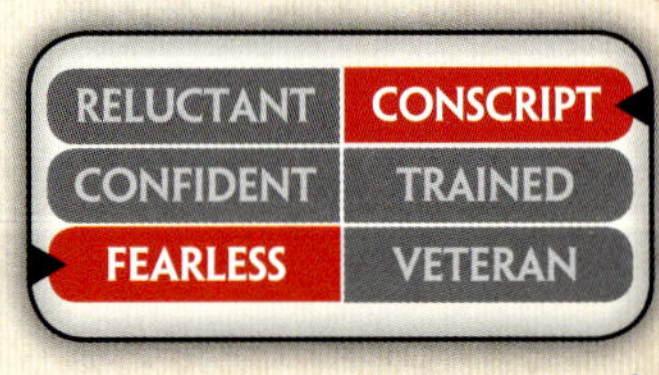

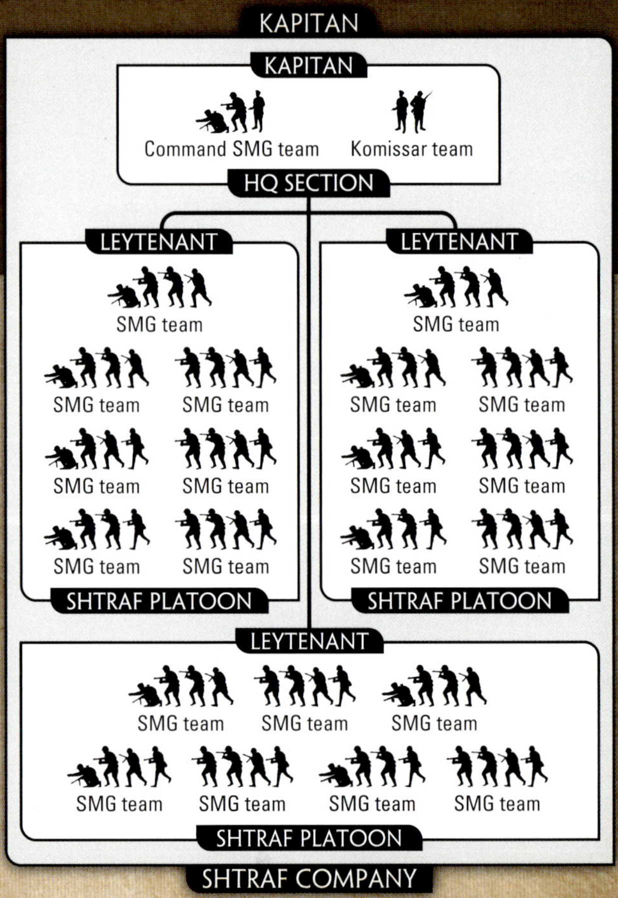

Shtraf Companies

Stalin's infamous Order 227—Not One Step Back—formed *Shtrafniye Roti* or Penal Companies in each Army. These were used as assault troops on risky operations where they could redeem themselves through combat. The soldiers of the Shtraf Company can only gain pardon for their crimes with their blood, so they tend to be hard to stop.

In *Flames Of War* adding a Shtraf Company is a good way of guaranteeing you force Always Attack in any mission. A Shtraf Company in never dug in or in Prepared Positions. However, a Shtraf Company always passes a Motivation Test on a roll of 2+, and they are totally ignored when taking a Company Morale Check. For the full Shtraf Company rules see page 251 of the *Flames Of War* rulebook.

CORPS SUPPORT

RELUCTANT | CONSCRIPT
CONFIDENT | TRAINED
FEARLESS | VETERAN

AIR SUPPORT

PRIORITY AIR SUPPORT

Il-2 Shturmovik	270 points

LIMITED AIR SUPPORT

Il-2 Shturmovik	200 points

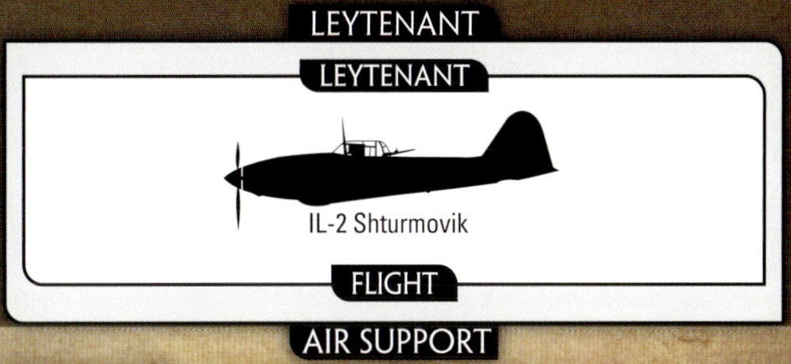

ASSAULT GUN COMPANY

COMPANY

5 SU-76M	185 points
4 SU-76M	150 points
3 SU-76M	115 points
4 SU-122	170 points
3 SU-122	130 points

OPTION

- Mount SMG Tank Escorts on all assault guns for +10 points per assault gun.

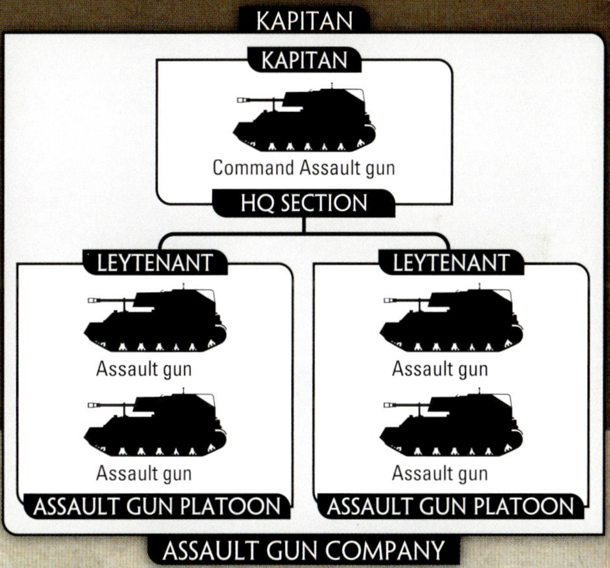

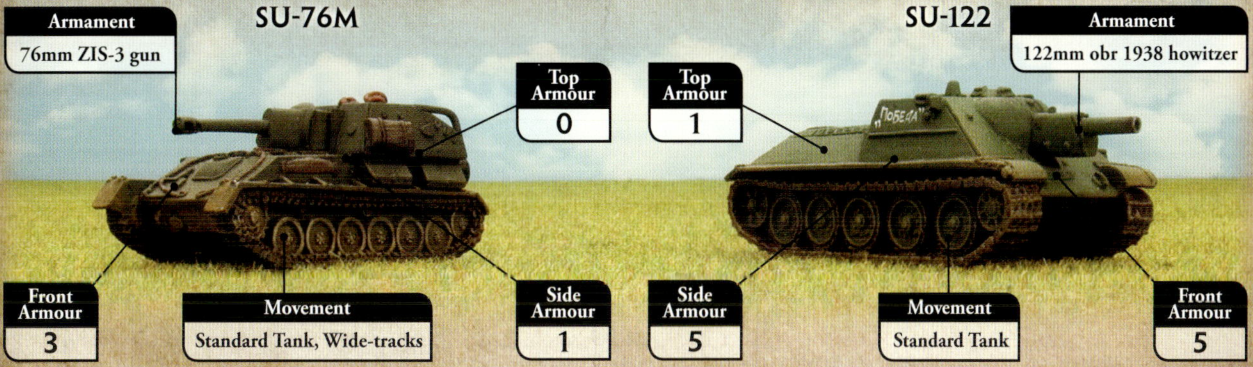

Weapon	Range	ROF	AT	FP	Notes
76mm ZIS-3 gun	32"/80cm	2	9	3+	Hull mounted.

Weapon	Range	ROF	AT	FP	Notes
122mm obr 1938 howitzer	24"/60cm	2	10	2+	Breakthrough gun, Hull mounted.

Guards Heavy Tank Company

Company

5 IS-2	675 points
4 IS-2	540 points
3 IS-2	405 points

- Arm any or all IS-2 tanks with .50 cal AA MG for +5 points per tank.

5 KV-85	555 points
4 KV-85	445 points
3 KV-85	335 points

5 KV-1s	425 points
4 KV-1s	340 points
3 KV-1s	255 points

Option

- Mount SMG Tank Escorts on all heavy tanks for +10 points per heavy tank.

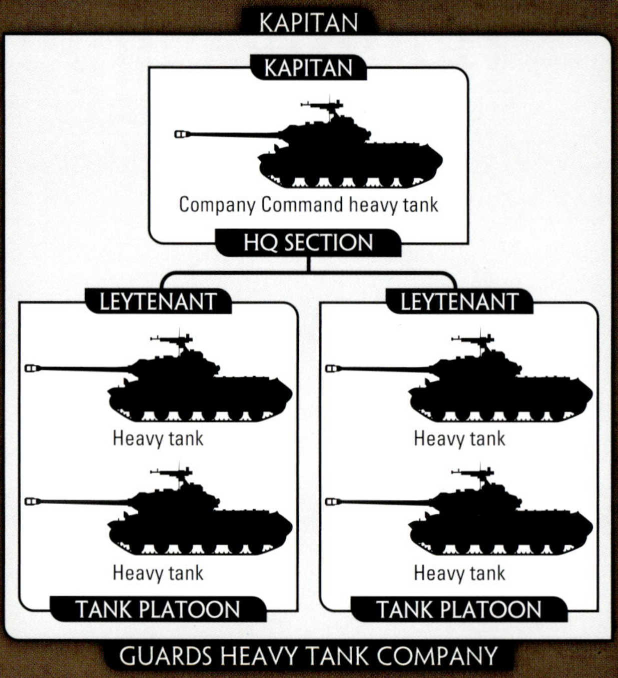

As one would expect Guards Heavy Tank Companies are Guards troops. As such they are always rated **Fearless Trained.**

With such a high proportion of officers in the company, Guards Heavy Tank Companies use more sophisticated tactics than most Soviet troops. They are not affected by the Hen and Chicks special rule.

Tank Escorts

While the tanks of the Red Army were sufficiently well armoured to be safe from most German anti-tank guns, losses to infantry tank-hunter teams were alarming. The Soviet solution was to protect the tanks with *tankodesantniki* (or tank riders, pronouced tan-ko-dye-sant-ni-ki), submachine-gun armed troops who ride to battle on the back of their tanks.

Tank Escorts are not teams in their own right. They are an addition to a Tank team that gives it extra capabilities. Tank teams with Tank Escorts roll To Hit with their escorts as well as the Tank team itself giving them two rolls to Hit in assaults in most circumstances. See the Tank Escorts rules on pages 200 to 201 of the *Flames Of War* rulebook.

IS-2

Weapon	Range	ROF	AT	FP	Notes
122mm D-25T gun	*32"/80cm*	*1*	*15*	*2+*	*Breakthrough gun.*

KV-85

Weapon	Range	ROF	AT	FP	Notes
85mm D-5T gun	*32"/80cm*	*2*	*12*	*3+*	

KV-1s

Weapon	Range	ROF	AT	FP	Notes
76mm F-34 gun	*32"/80cm*	*2*	*9*	*3+*	

Guards Heavy Assault Gun Company

Company

3 SU-152	235 points
2 SU-152	155 points
5 ISU-122	575 points
4 ISU-122	460 points
3 ISU-122	345 points
5 ISU-152	510 points
4 ISU-152	410 points
3 ISU-152	310 points

Options

- Arm any or all ISU-122 or ISU-152 assault guns with .50 cal AA MG for +5 points per assault gun.
- Mount SMG Tank Escorts on all assault guns for +10 points per assault gun.

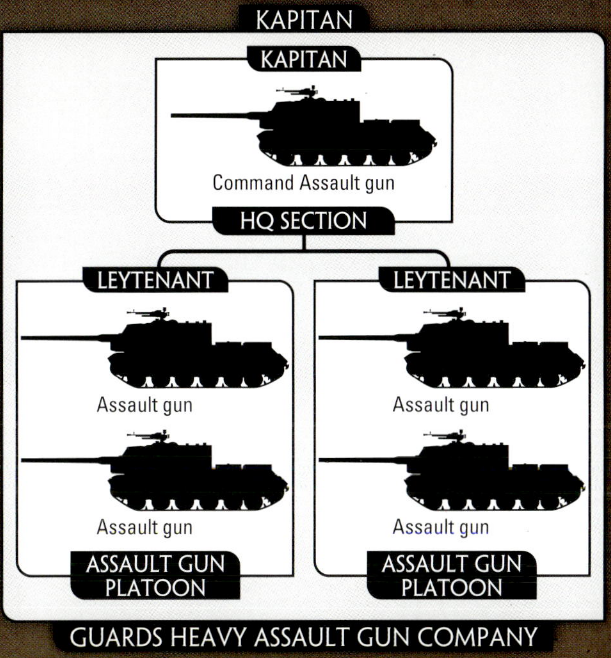

Guards Heavy Assault Gun Companies are Guards troops. As such they are always rated **Fearless Trained.**

RELUCTANT	CONSCRIPT
CONFIDENT	TRAINED
FEARLESS	VETERAN

Guards Heavy Assault Gun Companies use more sophisticated tactics than most Soviet troops. They are not affected by the Hen and Chicks special rule.

Volley Fire

When the Red Army came across a German strongpoint, assault guns and artillery batteries stopped to blast it using a massive centralised volley. If they did not move in the Movement Step, Gun teams and Turretless Tank teams may re-roll failed rolls To Hit when shooting at platoons within 16"/40cm (see page 250 of the *Flames Of War* rulebook).

Breakthrough Gun

Some weapons are just so powerful that there is no chance of surviving a hit from them. Infantry teams, Gun teams, and Unarmoured vehicles automatically fail their Saves when hit by a Breakthrough Gun or a Bunker Buster (see page 100 of the *Flames Of War* rulebook).

SU-152

Weapon	Range	ROF	AT	FP	Notes
152mm ML-20S gun	32"/80cm	1	13	1+	Bunker buster, Hull mounted.

ISU-122

Weapon	Range	ROF	AT	FP	Notes
122mm D-25S gun	32"/80cm	1	15	2+	Breakthrough gun, Hull mounted.

ISU-152

Weapon	Range	ROF	AT	FP	Notes
152mm ML-20S gun	32"/80cm	1	13	1+	Bunker buster, Hull mounted.

Sapper Company

Company

HQ Section with:

3 Sapper Platoons	270 points
2 Sapper Platoons	185 points
1 Sapper Platoon	100 points

Option

- Add Pioneer Supply horse-drawn wagon for +20 points, or a Pioneer Supply truck for +25 points.

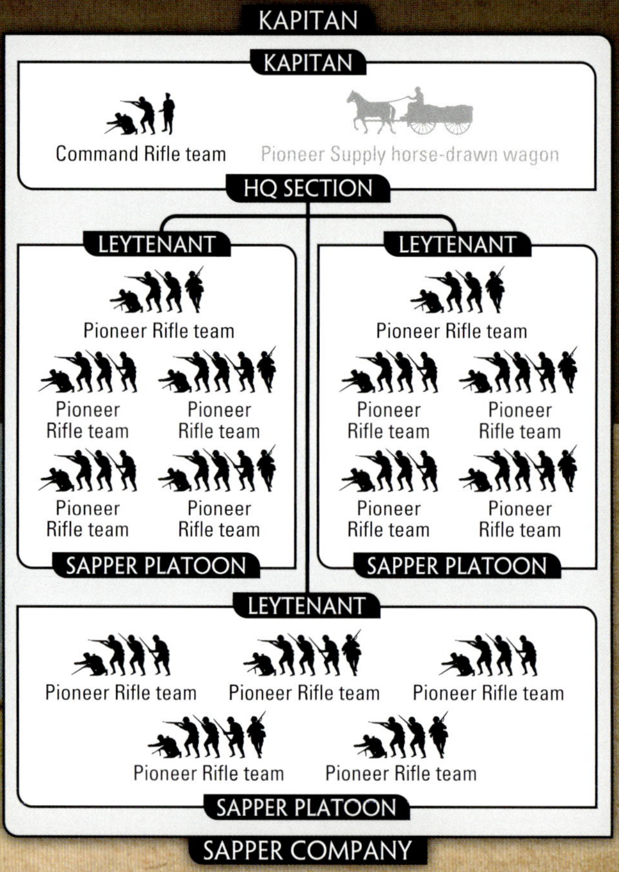

Tank Killer Company

Company

5 SU-85	300 points
4 SU-85	240 points
3 SU-85	180 points
5 SU-85M	365 points
4 SU-85M	290 points
3 SU-85M	215 points
5 SU-100	390 points
4 SU-100	310 points
3 SU-100	230 points

Option

- Give all assault guns SMG Tank Escorts for +10 points per tank.

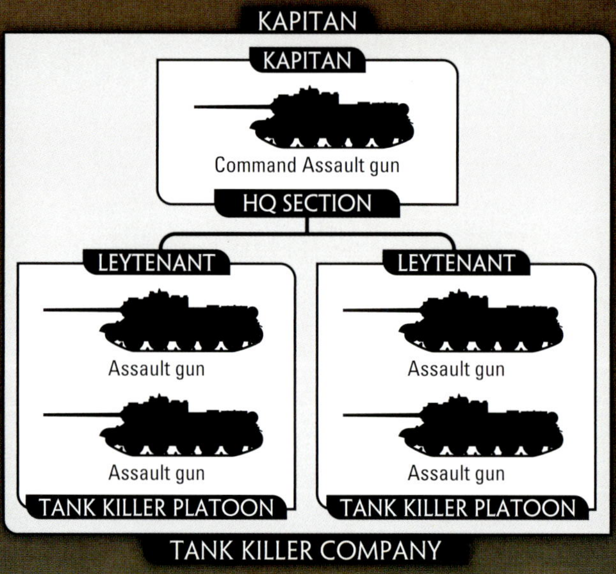

Weapon	Range	ROF	AT	FP	Notes
85mm D-5S gun	*32"/80cm*	*2*	*12*	*3+*	*Hull mounted.*

Weapon	Range	ROF	AT	FP	Notes
85mm D-5S gun	*32"/80cm*	*2*	*12*	*3+*	*Hull mounted.*

Artillery Battalion

Company

HQ Section with:

8 76mm ZIS-3 field guns and 4 122mm obr 1938	270 points
8 76mm ZIS-3 field guns	210 points
4 76mm ZIS-3 field guns and 4 122mm obr 1938	250 points
4 76mm ZIS-3 field guns	125 points
4 122mm obr 1938	140 points

Options

- Add Observer Rifle team for +15 points.
- Add PTRD anti-tank rifle teams to Howitzer Platoons for +10 points per team.
- Add horse-drawn wagon, horse-drawn limbers, and Stalinets tractors for +5 points for the battalion.

SU-100

Weapon	Range	ROF	AT	FP	Notes
100mm D-10S gun	40"/100cm	1	16	2+	Hull mounted

Reserve Heavy Artillery Battalion

Company

HQ Section with:

8 122mm obr 1938 howitzers	235 points
4 122mm obr 1938 howitzers	140 points
8 152mm obr 1943 howitzers	310 points
4 152mm obr 1943 howitzers	180 points

Options

- Add Observer Rifle team for +15 points.
- Add Stalinets tractors for +5 points for the battalion.

You may not field a Reserve Heavy Artillery Battalion unless you are fielding an Artillery Battalion (page 95) with at least four 122mm obr 1938 howitzers and as many guns in total; or a Motostrelkovy Artillery Battalion (page 84) with at least as many guns.

122mm obr 1938 Howitzer

Equipment: Gun shield

Notes: Breakthrough gun

Movement: Immobile

Weapon	Range	ROF	AT	FP
122mm obr 1938 howitzer	24"/60cm	1	7	2+
Firing bombardments	80"/200cm	-	4	3+

152mm obr 1943 Howitzer

Notes: Bunker buster

Equipment: Gun shield

Movement: Immobile

Weapon	Range	ROF	AT	FP
152mm obr 1943 howitzer	24"/60cm	1	10	1+
Firing bombardments	80"/200cm	-	5	2+

Guards Rocket Mortar Battalion

Company

HQ Section with:

8 BM-13 Katyusha	225 points
4 BM-13 Katyusha	140 points
2 BM-13 Katyusha	80 points

Option

- Model BM-13 Katyusha rocket launchers with five or more crew and count each rocket launcher as two weapons when firing a bombardment for +10 points per Rocket Mortar Platoon.

A Guards Rocket Mortar Battalion is rated as **Fearless Trained.**

RELUCTANT	CONSCRIPT
CONFIDENT	TRAINED
FEARLESS	VETERAN

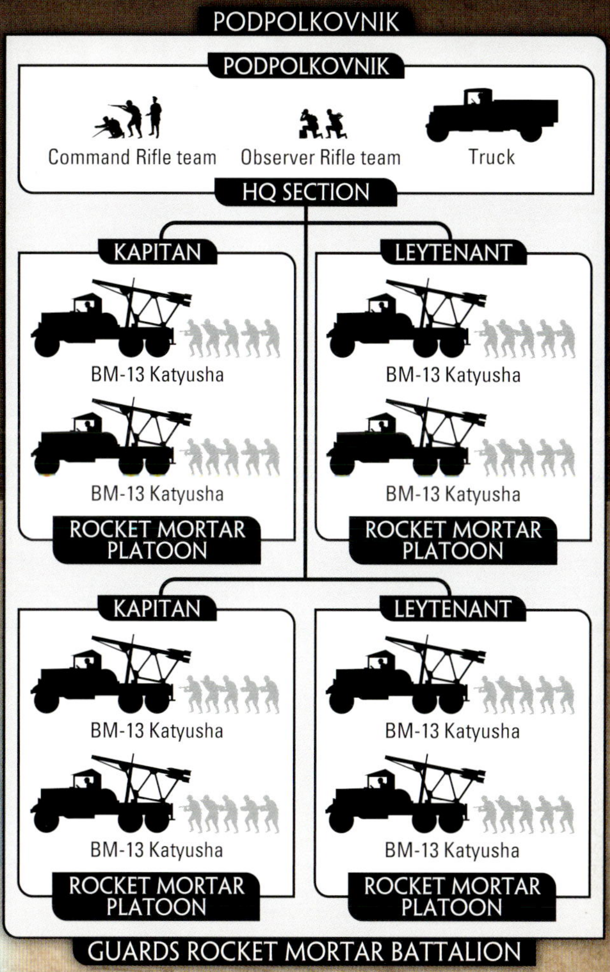

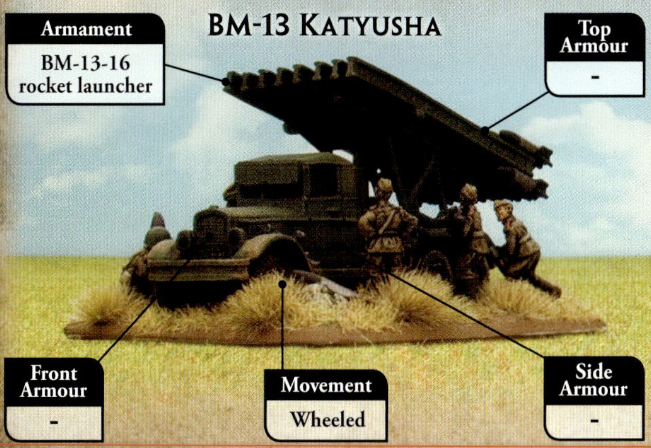

Weapon	Range	ROF	AT	FP	Notes
BM-13-16 rocket launcher	*64"/160cm*	*-*	*2*	*4+*	*Rocket launcher.*

Rocket Launchers

Salvo rocket launchers fire bombardments just like any other artillery, but with one key difference. After ranging in as usual (usually by firing a single rocket at a time, just like ordinary artillery), they fire all of their rockets in one massive salvo.

Bombardments fired by Rocket Launchers do not modify their To Hit rolls for Ranging In on the second or third attempt (see page 138 of the *Flames Of War* rulebook).

Tank Destruction Company

Company

HQ Section with:

4 45mm obr 1942 guns	90 points
2 45mm obr 1942 guns	50 points
4 76mm ZIS-3 anti-tank guns	90 points
2 76mm ZIS-3 anti-tank guns	50 points
4 57mm ZIS-2 guns	155 points
2 57mm ZIS-2 guns	80 points

Options

- Add PTRD anti-tank rifle team for +10 points.
- Add trucks for +5 points for the platoon.

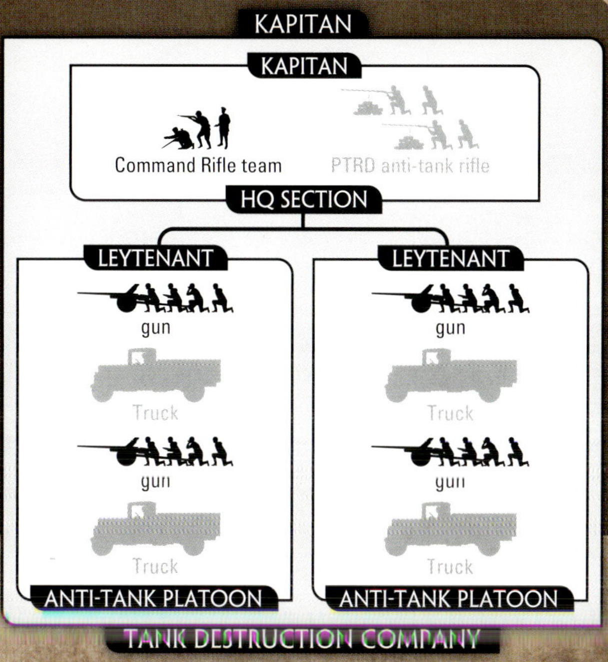

SOVIET ARSENAL

TANK TEAMS

Name *Weapon*	Mobility *Range*	Armour Front *ROF*	Side *Anti-tank*	Top *Firepower*	Equipment and Notes
LIGHT TANKS					
T-70 obr 1943	Standard Tank	4	2	1	Co-ax MG, Limited vision, Wide-tracks.
45mm obr 1938 gun	*24"/60cm*	*1*	*7*	*4+*	
Mark III (Valentine II)	Slow Tank	6	5	1	Co-ax MG.
OQF 2 pdr gun	*24"/60cm*	*2*	*7*	*4+*	
Mark III (Valentine VIII)	Slow Tank	6	4	1	Protected ammo.
OQF 6 pdr gun	*24"/60cm*	*2*	*10*	*4+*	
MEDIUM TANKS					
T-34 obr 1942	Standard Tank	6	5	1	Co-ax MG, Hull MG, Fast tank, Limited vision, Wide-tracks.
76mm F-34 gun	*32"/80cm*	*2*	*9*	*3+*	
T-34/85 obr 1943	Standard Tank	7	5	1	Co-ax MG, Hull MG, Limited vision.
85mm D-5T gun	*32"/80cm*	*2*	*12*	*3+*	
HEAVY TANKS					
KV-1s	Standard Tank	8	6	2	Co-ax MG, Hull MG, Turret-rear MG, Wide-tracks.
76mm F-34 gun	*32"/80cm*	*2*	*9*	*3+*	
KV-85	Slow Tank	9	7	2	Co-ax MG, Turret-rear MG.
85mm D-5T gun	*32"/80cm*	*2*	*12*	*3+*	
IS-2	Slow Tank	10	8	2	Co-ax MG, Turret-rear MG.
122mm D-25T gun	*32"/80cm*	*1*	*15*	*2+*	*Breakthrough gun.*
ASSAULT GUNS					
SU-76M	Standard Tank	3	1	0	Wide-tracks.
76mm ZIS-3 gun	*32"/80cm*	*2*	*9*	*3+*	*Hull mounted.*
SU-85	Standard Tank	5	5	1	
85mm D-5S gun	*32"/80cm*	*2*	*12*	*3+*	*Hull mounted.*
SU-85M	Slow Tank	9	5	1	Overloaded.
85mm D-5S gun	*32"/80cm*	*2*	*12*	*3+*	*Hull mounted.*
SU-100	Slow Tank	9	5	1	Overloaded.
100mm D-10S gun	*40"/100cm*	*1*	*16*	*2+*	*Hull mounted.*
SU-122	Standard Tank	5	5	1	
122mm obr 1938 howitzer	*24"/60cm*	*2*	*10*	*2+*	*Breakthrough gun, Hull mounted.*
SU-152	Slow Tank	7	6	2	
152mm ML-20S gun	*32"/80cm*	*1*	*13*	*1+*	*Bunker buster, Hull mounted.*
ISU-122	Slow Tank	9	7	2	
122mm D-25S gun	*32"/80cm*	*1*	*15*	*2+*	*Breakthrough gun, Hull mounted.*
ISU-152	Slow Tank	9	7	2	
152mm ML-20S gun	*32"/80cm*	*1*	*13*	*1+*	*Bunker buster, Hull mounted.*
ROCKET LAUNCHERS					
BM-13 Katyusha	Wheeled	-	-	-	
BM-13-16 rocket launcher	*64"/160cm*	-	*2*	*4+*	*Rocket launcher.*
VEHICLE MACHINE-GUNS					
Vehicle MG	*16"/40cm*	*3*	*2*	*6*	*ROF 1 if other weapons fire.*
.50 cal Vehicle MG	*16"/40cm*	*3*	*4*	*5+*	*ROF 1 if other weapons fire.*

Gun Teams

Weapon	Mobility	Range	ROF	Anti-tank	Firepower	Notes
PTRD anti-tank rifle	Man-packed	16"/40cm	2	5	5+	Tank Assault 3.
Maksim HMG	Man-packed	24"/60cm	6	2	6	ROF 3 when pinned down or moving.
82-BM-41 mortar	Man-packed	24"/60cm	2	2	3+	Minimum range 8"/20cm.
Firing bombardments		40"/100cm	-	2	6	
120-PM-38 mortar	Light	56"/140cm	-	3	3+	
76mm obr 1927 gun	Light	16"/40cm	2	5	3+	Gun shield.
Firing bombardments		64"/160cm	-	3	6	
45mm obr 1942 gun	Light	24"/60cm	3	8	4+	Gun shield.
57mm ZIS-2 gun	Heavy	32"/80cm	3	11	4+	Gun shield.
76mm ZIS-3 anti-tank gun	Heavy	32"/80cm	2	9	3+	Gun shield.
76mm ZIS-3 field gun	Heavy	32"/80cm	2	9	3+	Gun shield.
Firing bombardments		80"/200cm	-	3	6	
122mm obr 1938 howitzer	Immobile	24"/60cm	1	7	2+	Breakthrough gun, Gun shield.
Firing bombardments		80"/200cm	-	4	3+	
152mm obr 1943 howitzer	Immobile	24"/60cm	1	10	1+	Bunker buster, Gun shield.
Firing bombardments		80"/200cm	-	5	2+	

Infantry Teams

Team	Range	ROF	Anti-tank	Firepower	Weapons and Notes
Rifle team	16"/40cm	1	2	6	
Rifle/MG team	16"/40cm	2	2	6	
SMG team	4"/10cm	3	1	6	Full ROF when moving.
Flame-thrower team	4"/10cm	4	-	6	Flame-thrower.
Komissar team	4"/10cm	1	1	6	
Observer Rifle team	16"/40cm	1	2	6	Observer
Staff team			cannot shoot		Moves as a Heavy Gun team.

Additional Training and Equipment

Pioneer teams are Tank Assault 4.

Transport Teams

Vehicle	Mobility	Armour Front	Armour Side	Armour Top	Equipment and Notes
ZIS-5 3-ton, ZIS-6 4-ton, Dodge 3/4-ton, or Studebekker 21/2-ton truck	Wheeled	-	-	-	
Stalinets tractor	Slow Tank	-	-	-	
Horse-drawn wagon or limber	Horse-drawn	-	-	-	

Aircraft

Aircraft	Weapon	To Hit	Anti-tank	Firepower	Notes
Il-2 Shturmovik	Cannon	3+	9	5+	Flying tank.
	Bombs	4+	5	1+	
	Rockets	3+	6	3+	

WHERE TO NEXT?

Now that you have picked your nation of choice and purchased your first platoon or two, the next stage is to probably pick a more battle specific intelligence briefing. For example, if you choose Germans do you want them to be fighting the Allies on the beaches of Normandy or against the Red bear in Russia?

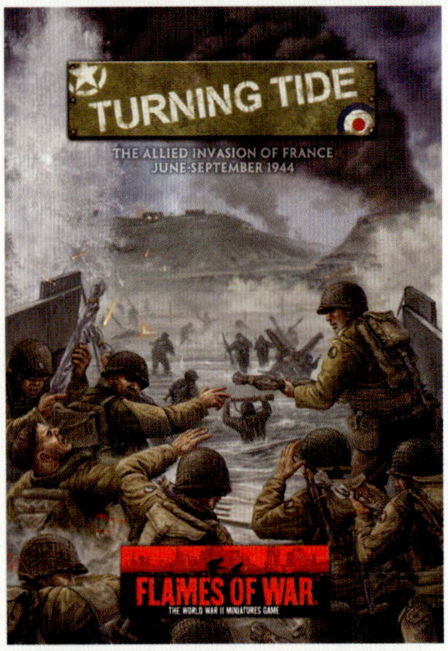

In the early morning darkness of 6 June 1944, the largest armada of ships the world has ever seen heaves to off the Normandy coastline. Aboard, thousands of Allied soldiers wait in readiness for their date with destiny.

Turning Tide is the definitive volume for anyone wishing to take command of the British and Americans as they fight off the beaches of Normandy into mainland Europe.

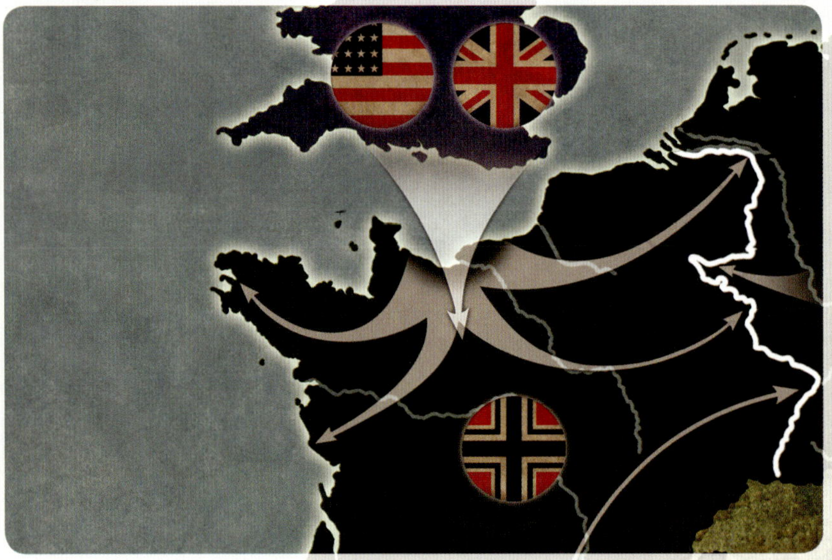

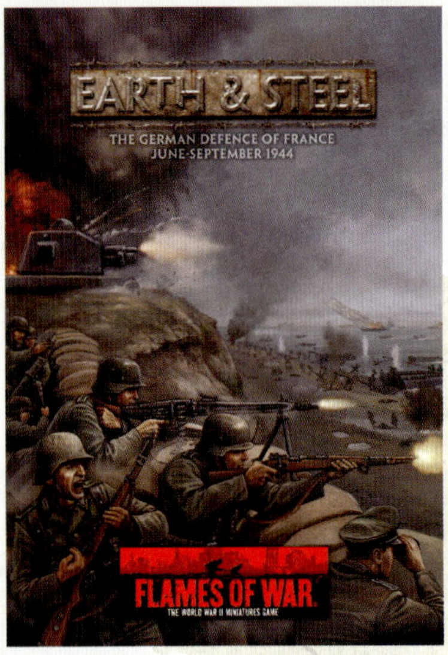

Opposing the Allied D-Day landings were the grenadiers and panzer troops of the German Seventh Army. The invaders were met on the beaches with withering fire from the defenders and a bloody battle ensued. Hard fought defence and vicious counterattacks would characterise the German struggle for Normandy in the following months.

Earth & Steel gives you all the equipment and Intelligence Briefings to stop the invasion. Take command of the Infantry on the beaches, or spearhead armoured counterattacks to throw the Allies back into the sea.

THE FLAMES OF WAR HOBBY

Now you have taken that first step into *Flames Of War* World War II miniature gaming, you will be wondering where to go next. *Flames Of War* provides many other things to help you along the road of your *Flames Of War* experience. There are plenty of other books providing many varied Intelligence Briefings offering an array of choices to the *Flames Of War* player. The miniatures range provides all the models and miniatures you will need to field theses forces. These are all packed conveniently with everything you need to field them in *Flames Of War*. The *Flames Of War* hobby range provide everything required to assemble and paint you models including tools, paints, brushes, bases, flock and other basing materials. To enhance your gaming experience pre-painted terrain, templates, tape measures and dice are also available. Don't forget to check out the *www.FlamesOfWar.com* website where you can talk to other gamers on the forum, read *Flames Of War* news, modelling, gaming and history articles, download free PDF Intelligence Briefings and learn about great new products. So get on out there and start playing *Flames Of War!*